OBJECTS AND DATABASES

G000093647

THE McGRAW-HILL
INTERNATIONAL SERIES IN SOFTWARE ENGINEERING

Consulting Editor

Professor D. Ince
The Open University

Titles in this Series

OBJECTS AND DATABASES

Petr Kroha

McGRAW-HILL BOOK COMPANY

London · New York · St Louis · San Francisco · Auckland
Bogotá · Caracas · Lisbon · Madrid · Mexico · Milan
Montreal · New Delhi · Panama · Paris · San Juan · São Paulo
Singapore · Sydney · Tokyo · Toronto

Published by
McGRAW-HILL Book Company Europe
SHOPPENHANGERS ROAD · MAIDENHEAD · BERKSHIRE · SL6 2QL, ENGLAND
TELEPHONE 0628 23432
FAX 0628 770224

British Library Cataloguing in Publication Data
Kroha, Petr
   Objects and Databases. – (McGraw-Hill
   International Series in Software
   Engineering)
   I. Title II. Series
   005.74

   ISBN 0–07–707790–3

Library of Congress Cataloging-in-Publication Data
Kroha, Petr,
   Objects and databases / Petr Kroha.
      p.   cm. – (McGraw-Hill international series in software engineering)
   Includes bibliographical references and index.
   ISBN 0–07–707790–3
   1. Object-oriented databases.   I. Title.   II. Series.
QA76.9.D3K738   1993
005.75 – dc20   93–9595
                                                              CIP

Copyright © 1993 McGraw-Hill International (UK) Limited. All rights reserved.
No part of this publication may be reproduced, stored in a retrieval system, or
transmitted, in any form or by any means, electronic, mechanical, photocopying,
recording, or otherwise, without the prior permission of McGraw-Hill International
(UK) Limited.

12345 CUP 9654

Typeset by Wyvern Typesetting Limited
and printed and bound in Great Britain by Page Bros, Norwich

CONTENTS

PREFACE

The objective of this book is to present the major features of object-oriented database systems in the context of existing problems and known methods for their solution. Since concepts such as data abstraction, encapsulation, inheritance and polymorphism are of fundamental importance to the topic, we will explain in detail how database technology uses them. We do this by discussing a series of examples that show the typical use of the relevant constructs. The examples are chosen on the basis of their suitability in illustrating specific features.

This book is written for programmers and advanced students who are assumed to have an elementary knowledge of programming and databases which will be strengthened by Part I. There are several ways in which the book can be used. The most obvious is for database programmers who have a good knowledge of a commercial database system (dBASE, ORACLE, etc.) gained from manuals and who need an introductory text that takes their experience into account (unlike many introductory texts) and that does not demand a deep knowledge of algebra (as do theoretical monographs). This book is especially suitable for those who refuse to believe that there are some applications where their preferred relational database systems would fail (in fact there are such applications). The sub-title of this book could be 'From dBASE to GemStone' because these systems are often used in examples illustrating and comparing different approaches of relational and object-oriented database systems. This book can be used as an advanced upper-level undergraduate or a graduate text in database technology as I have used it in my teaching.

The best way to study this text is to read it completely in the order it is presented. However, readers with an adequate knowledge of database management can omit Chapter 1. Also, those who are interested in only one of the query languages described in Part II can perhaps skip some of its chapters.

The book consists of four parts:

- The introductory Part I (Chapters 1–4) describes the basic features of database technology, the relational model, its shortcoming and extensions, and the properties of object-oriented database systems. This part motivates the need for object-oriented database management systems.
- Part II (Chapters 5–7) deals with the concepts of object-oriented programming important from the database point of view (Pascal, C++, Smalltalk and OPAL, LISP and AutoLISP) because C++, OPAL, and LISP are often used as query languages for object-oriented DBMSs.
- Part III (Chapters 8 and 9) describes the logical organization of an object-oriented database and its design, and finally
- Part IV (Chapters 10–13) deals with the implementation techniques used for this purpose and with perspectives of object-oriented database systems.

The aim of this book is to give a concise and readable explanation of object-oriented database management systems.

ACKNOWLEDGEMENTS

I would like to express my appreciation to people who helped me with my lectures and with this book. Above all, I wish to thank F. Haferkorn and R. Schneider for supporting my lectures at the Institute of Technology of Dortmund (Germany), H. Decker and H.-P. Schwefel for supporting my lectures at the University of Dortmund, N. Fuhr and W. Emmerich (University of Dortmund) for valuable comments and G. Gottlob (Technical University Vienna, Austria) for encouraging me. I am grateful to G. Schlageter (University of Hagen, Germany) for supporting my experimenting with GemStone, and A. Borghoff (CAD-Systems, Dortmund) for the touch of practice. Several of my students reviewed individual chapters and provided me with useful comments. I wish especially to thank R. Breker, M. Wayrauch, W. Krieg and D. Dong.

I started with object-oriented systems at the University of Linköping (Sweden) where I was supported by P. Fritzson, B. Lennartsson and S. Häglund.

Finally, I would like to thank John Milner (The City University, London), John Rankin (La Trobe University, Melbourne, Australia), and Jane Salusbury for patiently polishing my English. Special thanks should also go to the copyeditor, James Shepherd, and to all of the McGraw-Hill staff who worked on this book.

LIST OF TRADEMARKS

Ada is a trademark of the US Government (AJPO)

AutoLISP is a trademark of Autodesk Inc.

C is a trademark of Borland International Inc.

C++ is a trademark of Borland International Inc.

COBOL is a trademark of the US Department of Defense

dBASE is a trademark of Ashton-Tate Corporation

DB2 is a trademark of International Business Machines Corporation

FORTRAN is a trademark of Digital Research Inc.

FoxBASE is a trademark of Fox Software Inc.

GemStone is a trademark of Servio Logic Development Corporation

Informix is a trademark of Informix Corporation

INGRES is a trademark of the Ingres Corporation Inc.

Iris is a trademark of Hewlett-Packard Inc.

LISP is a trademark of The Massachusetts Institute of Technology (MIT)

O_2 is a trademark of O_2 Technology

Object Pascal is a trademark of Apple Computer Inc.

Objectivity DB is a trademark of Objectivity

ObjectStore is a trademark of ObjectDesign

ONTOS is a trademark of Ontologic Inc.

OPAL is a trademark of Servio Logic Development Corporation

OpenODB is a trademark of Hewlett-Packard Inc.

ORACLE is a trademark of Oracle Corporation UK Ltd

ORION is a trademark of Itasca

Paradox is a trademark of Borland International Inc.

Poet is a trademark of BKS Software

Smalltalk is a trademark of Rank Xerox Corporation

SUN is a trademark of Sun Microsystems, Inc.

Turbo Pascal is a trademark of Borland International Inc.

PART
ONE

INTRODUCTION

ONE

INTRODUCTION TO DATABASE TECHNOLOGY

This chapter is intended to introduce the basic ideas behind database systems and will be done principally through examples of very simple data processing problems. The intention is to convey an overall picture before presenting the factors leading to the use of object-oriented concepts in database technology. Of course, all the points illustrated here have already been covered in several books. Despite this, it is hoped that this overview will help the reader to see how the various constructs and examples given in subsequent chapters fit into an overall framework.

Before doing this, however, it will be necessary to discuss briefly what database systems development involves and to introduce some of the basic terminology.

1.1 PROBLEMS OF FILE PROCESSING SYSTEMS

In this section the main subject is data, which are facts concerning objects, events or other entities of the real world. By entity we denote a thing (an object of the real world) which exists and which can be distinguished from another entity. Data describes properties of entities, which are called attributes. Often, we can distinguish groups of 'similar' objects which are called entity sets. A programmer would say that an entity set consists of all entities of the same type. Since we always assume that we have not only one entity but potentially the whole entity set, we define attributes as properties of entity sets. Each attribute can obtain any attribute value from its domain. Domain is a set of values.

Information is data that has been organized or prepared in a form suitable for decision making. Therefore there is no sense in collecting data

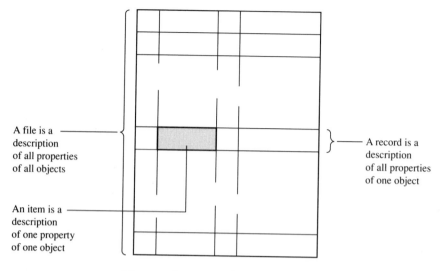

A file is a
description
of all properties
of all objects

An item is a
description
of one property
of one object

A record is a
description
of all properties
of one object

We mean relevant properties of relevant objects

Figure 1.1 Representation of facts in a file

without knowing what the information should be, i.e. what kind of
decision should be made. The first approach to data collection used in the
first computers was a file processing system.

For each entity (let us say for each object) we have one record whose
items each represent one attribute of the object and contain attribute
values. Records describing objects of the same type have the same size
and can be collected in a file (Fig. 1.1). Note that at this stage of knowledge
it is natural to have all the properties of one object stored together in one
unit (i.e. in one record of one file). In Chapter 2 we will show that this is
often not possible when using a relational database system.

All file processing systems used two basic methods: seeking and updating (Fig. 1.2). These were used to build application programs which determined how processing was to be done, and performed one or more related
tasks associated with the application. Information systems were constructed from sets of files and application programs in such a way that the
output file of one process was used as an input file for the next.

Many information systems built in this way are still running today, but
developers realized during the late sixties that there are basic limitations to
traditional file processing systems—uncontrolled redundancy, inconsistent
data, inflexibility, limited data sharing and security in multi-user
environments.

Uncontrolled redundancy is caused by the fact that each application
has its own files, which means that the same data may be stored

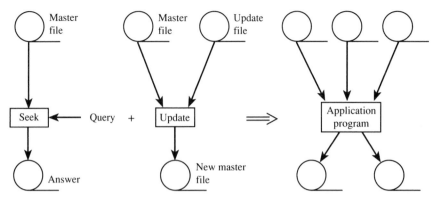

Figure 1.2 Basic methods of file processing

repeatedly. There are several disadvantages to recording the same data item in multiple files. First, storage space is wasted. Second, the same data may have to be input several times to update all occurrences of the data item.

Example
We have an information system with data about employees. Miss X gets married. She now becomes Mrs Y. We must change her name in all files. But she also changes her address (and perhaps the colour of her hair, her bank account, etc.). When we perform these updates we will reach a state where $(k-1)$ files are updated, the kth file is just processed and the last $(k+1, \ldots, n)$ files contain the old name and address. When an application program uses one of the updated files and one of the non-updated files at the same time it will discover that Mrs Y has two different addresses. This is an inconsistent state of data in an information system. The system does not know where to send congratulations on her marriage.

Inconsistency of data is inevitable when the same data is stored in multiple locations. The only way to prevent inconsistency is to lock all data which prevents other users or applications from accessing it until the update is complete (the concept of a transaction will be given later). This is very difficult when the files are directly controlled by different users, so there is a strong likelihood that some files will reflect the old data, while others reflect the new. Inconsistencies in stored data are one of the most common sources of errors in computer applications. They undermine the confidence of the user in the integrity of the information system.

Data integrity denotes a state of data where it precisely reflects a snapshot in time of a reality with all semantic relationships intact and consistent.

The idea of a file processing system is based on the assumption that its inputs and outputs were anticipated in the original design of the system. Since demands are changing, such systems are often quite inflexible and cannot easily respond to requests that were not anticipated in the original design. For every new format of the output information a new application program must be written.

Example
A clerk in a personnel department has to write a list of employees having a lorry driver's licence and being less than 40 years old. He has an application program for listing all employees with a driver's licence and one for listing all employees younger than a given age, so he has two possibilities. First, he can perform manually the necessary operation with the two lists. Second, he can ask a programmer to write a new application program. The day after this application program is ready the clerk has to write a list of employees with a lorry driver's licence, who are less than 40 years old and who speak Spanish. The whole procedure must then be repeated.

With redundancy and consistency, a problem of sharing data is related. In the traditional file processing applications approach each application has its own private files, and there is little opportunity for users to share data outside of their own applications. It is difficult to update files with duplicate data, and it is also difficult for the designer, when developing new applications, to exploit data contained in existing files. Instead, new files are designed that duplicate much of the existing data.

Applications written for file processing systems are expensive. Programmers must master a very detailed programming language such as COBOL. They must design each record and file, select file access methods to be used and write procedures specifying data manipulation. Every application program is an individual product of the art of programming. However, changes will take place during the lifetime of the application program. Any modification to a data file or any new customer's request requires that the program be modified. This process is referred to as program maintenance. It is known that 80 per cent of programming effort is devoted to this activity. Of course, programmers sometimes take better jobs at other companies, so it is very often the case that programmers are maintaining a system that they have not written.

1.2 MAIN IDEAS OF THE DATABASE APPROACH

These problems led to the database approach. A database is a collection of interrelated data and the aim of its design is to answer queries from

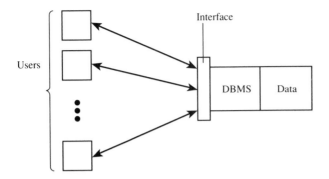

Figure 1.3 Main idea of the database approach

users. It is integrated in that the redundancy is eliminated (as much as possible), and it is shared by users in that they can use it simultaneously or at least pseudo-simultaneously. The principles and main ideas of the database approach to data processing corresponds to the concept of abstract data types.

Data in a database is manipulated exclusively by a system of programs called a database management system (DBMS). This system is created by a vendor as a tool to implement databases and applications. The user can access data only through the services of the DBMS. This service is defined as a user interface (Fig. 1.3). There are defined data types, data variables and access methods (statements) for this purpose. Implementation details are hidden, i.e. data description is separated from application programs. Users of the DBMS can use the predefined types, variables and procedures (methods). Some of these methods serve to define new data objects (the types are predefined) and some can be used as statements when creating new user-defined methods.

Very often there are many interfaces to the DBMS (Fig. 1.4). We can divide users into groups based on the interface they use as follows:

- A database administrator who has complete responsibility for the database and for establishing controls on accessing, updating, and protecting data.
- Application programmers using high-level languages.
- Application programmers using the languages of the DBMS.
- Non-professional users using a simple query language.
- Naive users using an application interface for working with a fixed application.

Every DBMS interface for applications includes a data definition language (DDL) for a description of processing objects, a data manipulation language (DML) for a description of algorithms on these objects,

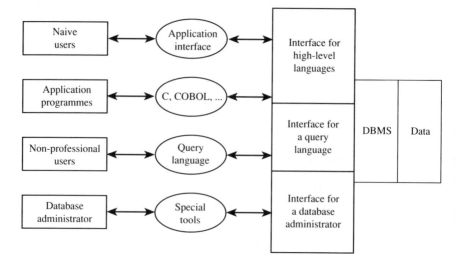

Figure 1.4 Interfaces to a DBMS

and a data control language (DCL) for a description of access privileges to objects.

All definitions are stored in a data dictionary. This is in fact a database of definitions. Since there is no standard, data dictionaries have different structures. However, most of them contain descriptions of fields, files, schema, subschemata, transactions, reports, screen, programs, users, etc. The use of the data dictionary in query processing is shown in Fig. 1.5.

Simple database systems do not have a centralized data dictionary. For example, dBASE stores definitions of columns in headings of each file representing a relation (a data table). In recent versions, a catalog can be used which contains descriptions of logically related files. Obviously, this catalog is far from being a data dictionary.

Data catalogs of a SQL-based database system contain the following tables:

- SYSCATALOG (for each table: user name, number of columns)
- SYSCOLUMNS (for each column: table name, type, etc.)
- SYSINDEXES (for each index: table name, key of sorting, etc.)
- SYSUSERAUTH (for each user: name, password, access privileges)
- SYSVIEWS (for each view: view definition).

Such a catalog can be seen as a subset of a data dictionary.

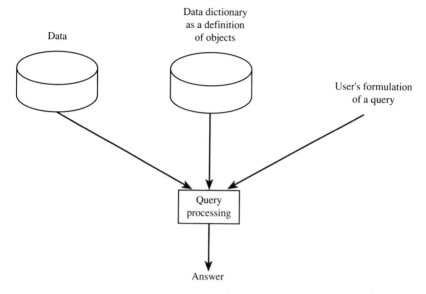

Figure 1.5 A data dictionary in DBMS

1.3 LOGICAL ORGANIZATION

1.3.1 Data and Models

Before using any database language we must have an abstract model of our problem. This model presents an abstraction of reality that can be systematically manipulated (Fig. 1.6.) Using this model, we obtain a set of definitions describing the part of reality in which we are interested. Entity sets and their attributes will then be represented by defined types and their instances.

Every entity set must possess at least one attribute (or several in combination) to distinguish its entities from each other. This unique set of attributes of an entity set is called an identifier. Identifiers are represented by keys. Each entity of an entity set must have a different value for the key. Besides entities—entity sets and their attributes—we also have relationships between two or more entity sets. These relationships can also have attributes. Relationships are uniquely identified by the keys of the participating entity sets.

When modelling, we first have to describe in its entirety the part of reality in which we are interested. Thus we obtain a conceptual model— a schema (Fig. 1.7). This defines the entire information resource at an abstract level and it is the basis for design of the implementation in DDL, DML and DCL. Only the database administrator typically needs a view

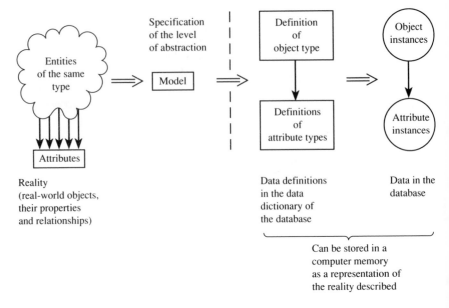

Figure 1.6 Model and abstractions

of the entire database. Each qualified user requires a different view of the data — a subschema.

1.3.2 E–R model

There are many models used in database systems. We now consider the entity–relationship model, which is very representational and is used primarily as a database design method. It is intended as a notation for conceptual schema design, but note that this model does not include a notation of operations on data, so the conceptual model cannot be completely described by the E–R model.

The E–R model uses entity–relationship diagrams, where:

- Rectangles represent entity sets
- Ovals represent attributes
- Diamonds represent relationships

These graphical elements are linked together to represent the model.

In Fig. 1.8 we see the entity sets Teacher, and Subject, which are related by the relationship Teaches. Each entity set has its key (Code_T for Teacher) and its attributes. The relationship Teaches has its own attribute.

The model given is very representational but not complete. We can

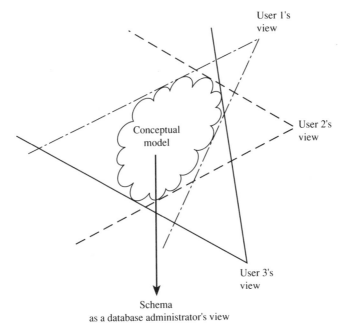

Figure 1.7 Schema and views

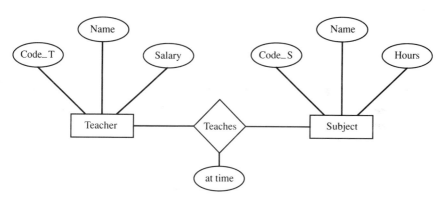

Figure 1.8 The E–R model

imagine four possible interpretations of the relationship Teaches in Fig. 1.8:

- Each teacher teaches (at most) one subject and no subject is taught by more than one teacher (mapping one-to-one).
- Each teacher teaches one or more subjects but no subject is taught by more than one teacher (mapping one-to-many).

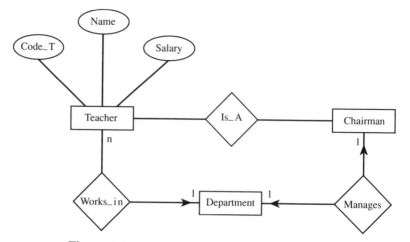

Figure 1.9 Relationship one-to-one and many-to-one

- Each teacher teaches (at most) one subject and one subject can be taught by more teachers (mapping many-to-one).
- Each teacher teaches more than one subject and one subject can be taught by more than one teacher (mapping many-to-many).

We can say that for every relationship there is a mapping among entity sets (Fig. 1.9). Edges with directions indicated by arrows are used for classifying relationships.

When a relationship R is many-to-one from A to B, we place an edge with an arrow from the diamond for R to the rectangle for B.

Example
Many teachers work in a department but each works in only one (i.e. in this one) department. This is a many-to-one relationship from Teacher to Department.

When a relationship R is one-to-one from A to B we place arrows from R to both A and B.

Example
Each department has only one chairman and each chairman manages only one department. This is a one-to-one relationship. We place an arrow from Manages to Chairman and from Manages to Department.

When a relationship R is many-to-many, no arrows are used. We have seen such a relationship (Teaches) in Fig. 1.8. The relationship Teaches has its own attribute, whose value specifies a property of each pair of entities Teacher–Subject which belongs to the relationship Teaches.

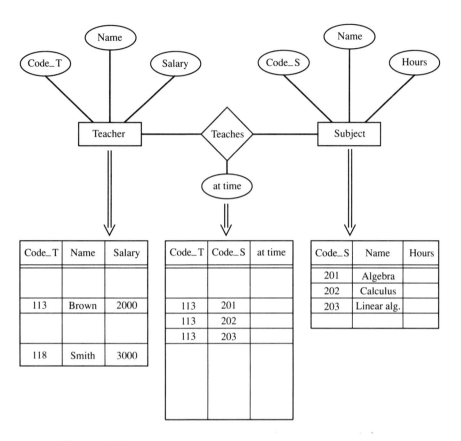

Figure 1.10 The E–R model and its implementation using only tables

1.4 DATA MODELS AND THEIR PHYSICAL ORGANIZATION

We will consider problems of modelling in more depth in Chapter 8. At this point, it is worth enquiring about the possibilities of implementation. First, we apply a programmer's point of view; then, in Sec. 1.5, we show a mathematician's point of view.

At first, we have two different simple methods to implement relationships. In Fig. 1.10 we see that we can implement an entity set as a table, where each column represents an attribute, each row represents one entity (i.e. one tuple of its attribute values) in the current instance, and each element of the table represents the value of given attribute for a given entity. Each entity in the table is identified by the value of the key-attribute of the entity set. This key-attribute consists of one or more columns that, as a group, must have no repeated values. A relationship can be described in the same way except that, for identification, we have to use the keys of related entity sets, i.e. we must specify 'who has the relationship with whom'.

Since an E–R model contains only entity sets, relationships and their attributes, we have succeeded in implementing this model exclusively with tables. We can decide that the elements of a table (as components of objects) can be of types Number, String and Date, and we have a very simple but useful implementation. The conversion from an E–R model to a set of tables can be carried out automatically.

In database programming we are especially interested in persistent objects, i.e. in those which outlast the lifetime of the running application program that has created and used them. A major advantage of the table-oriented implementation given above is that there is a simple way to represent tables as persistent objects. Every programmer sees the way: we can implement every table as a file. Every entity will be represented by a record and every value of its attributes by an item. In the rest of this book we will use interchangeably (depending on context) the terms a tuple of attribute values, a row of a table representing an entity set, and a record of a file containing attribute values.

This is how simple database systems for microcomputers are designed (e.g. dBASE, etc.). Many database systems are more complex programs, so what we mean here by a simple database system is dBASE IV version 1.1, for example, which needs 7 MB on the hard disk for installation.

The next method of implementing the E–R model is simply to use pointers to represent relationships (Fig. 1.11). We append a pointer part to every record representing an entity (Fig. 1.12). In this pointer part we will write addresses (or key values) of related records.

We can extract two important characteristics from Figs. 1.10 and 1.11. When a relationship is represented by a table then we have the following disadvantages and advantages:

- *Disadvantage* We have redundant values for the teacher's code code_T. It is necessary to represent the mapping of one-teacher-to-many-subjects in this way.
- *Advantage* We can use not only mapping but also relations for modelling relationships. We can freely append new rows to the table representing the relationship because a table (a file) is a flexible data structure in the sense that we can freely increase the number of rows (records).

When a relationship is represented by a system of pointers we have:

- *Disadvantages* We have a fixed number of pointers in the pointer part of each record type. We cannot append an increasing number of subjects to one teacher because a file is not a flexible data structure in the sense of changeable record size. We no longer have a one-data-type system when accessing entity sets and entities.

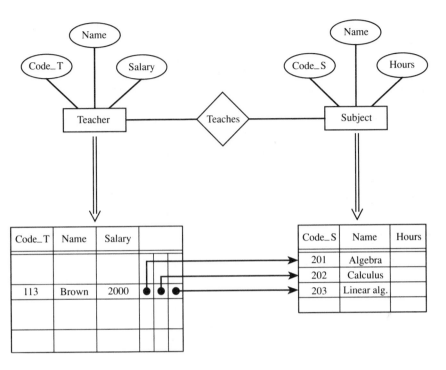

Figure 1.11 The E–R model and its implementation using records and pointers

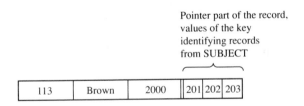

Figure 1.12 The pointer part of a record representing an entity

- *Advantage* We do not need so much memory space, because the values of the keys are not stored redundantly. We can directly access the records we are looking for, i.e. we do not need to search the table representing the relationship.

1.5 THE TABLE-ORIENTED IMPLEMENTATION AND THE RELATIONAL MODEL

In this section we show a mathematician's point of view of the table-only-oriented solution of a representation E–R model as described in

Sec. 1.4. The idea of representing all data in a database as a set of tables leads to the concept of a relational model. Although this concept was not used in the first database implementations it is very suitable for explaining the elementary principles. There are some well-known and very widely used database systems built more or less on this idea (e.g. dBASE, FoxBASE, Clipper, Paradox, ORACLE, INGRES, Informix, DB2). Altogether, there may be more than a million installations beginning with dBASE II under CP/M, with dBASE IV on the IBM PC, continuing on workstations with Informix under UNIX, up to mainframes using ORACLE and DB2.

We will start with the mathematical concept underlying the relational model. This is based on set theory.

We begin by mapping what is intuitively known in a simple form, as in Fig. 1.13. We can describe a mapping from a set A to a set B as a set of tuples, where the first element in each tuple is an element of the set A and the second element in each tuple is an element of the set B. To extend this concept to more than two sets (e.g. k sets), we first define the Cartesian product as the set of all k-tuples $(v_1, v_2, \ldots, v_k)$ such that v_1 is in

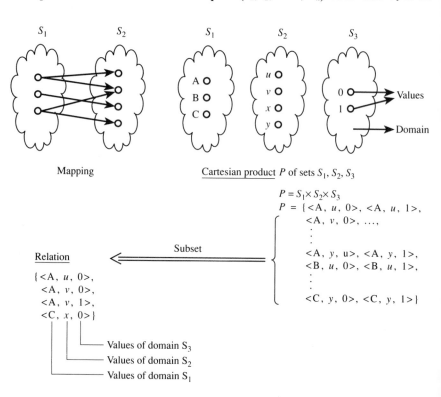

Figure 1.13 A relation as a subset of the Cartesian product

S_1, v_2 is in S_2, and so on. Sets S_1, S_2, . . ., S_k are called domains. In a non-mathematical way, we could say that the combinations of domain values consist of all possible combinations of values such that the given order in each tuple is preserved, i.e. the first element of the created tuple is always a value from the first domain, etc. (Fig. 1.14).

A relation is defined as a subset of the Cartesian product, i.e. we do not use all combinations of domain values, but only those describing the values of the attributes of our entities. Each tuple of a relation is called a member of the relation. The arity or degree of a relation denotes how many attributes (components) its tuples have.

Like entity sets, relations have components that can serve as keys. What attribute of an entity set (i.e. a component of a relation) will be considered the key depends on the modelled reality, on the schema. More than one group of attributes can have this property. All such groups of attributes are called candidate keys. Which candidate key will be used as the identifier is a design decision made by the database designer. It cannot be deduced from more basic principles, because it depends on how the database will be used.

In the previous paragraphs we described the mathematical notation of

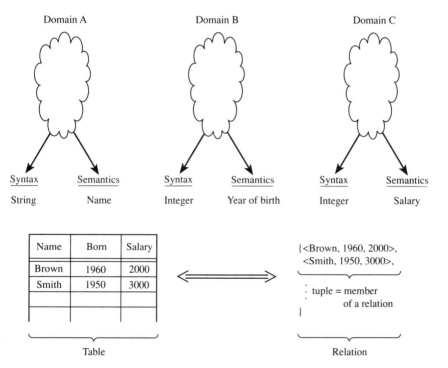

Figure 1.14 Domains, relations, tables

a relation. More profitable would be the introduction of the family of operations usually associated with the relational model. In this book we shall consider only the SQL approach. This is used as a query language in many relational database systems (from dBASE IV, Informix, and ORACLE to DB2) and its extension has a good chance of becoming a query language for object-oriented DBMS. We will introduce here the following operations:

- Selection
- Projection
- Join
- Equi-join
- Union
- Difference
- Intersection

Selection (sometimes called restriction) retrieves all tuples of a specified relation that satisfy a certain condition and constructs a new relation that contains the selected tuples (Fig. 1.15). It is assumed that a primary key access method has been implemented to make query processing more efficient. In table-oriented terminology we would say that selection constructs a new table by taking a horizontal subset of an existing table, i.e. it retrieves a specified subset of rows.

Projection (Fig. 1.15) retrieves all tuples of a specified relation but

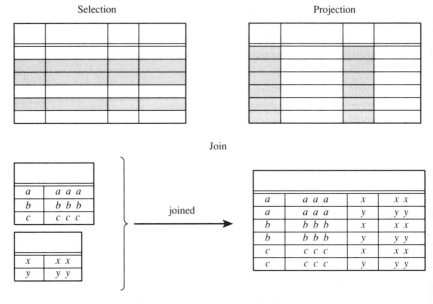

Figure 1.15 Selection, projection and join

includes in each tuple of the newly constructed relation only those attributes identified by name. During this process it can happen that some tuples will be identical because the distinguishing component has been omitted by projection. Since this mechanism is based on set theory where identical elements in a set are not permitted, some tuples can be lost. In table-oriented terminology we would say that projection forms a vertical subset of an existing table by extracting specified columns from all rows to form a new table. If only some of the keys are extracted the resultant table could contain duplicate rows. Some DML operators automatically eliminate this redundancy.

Join (Fig. 1.15) denotes an operation which provides a Cartesian product of relations. Relations are sets and the Cartesian product of relations is the same as the Cartesian product of sets except that the domains are themselves sets of tuples, i.e. it creates 'super tuples' where the first element is a tuple from the first domain, the second element is a tuple from the second domain, etc., in all combinations. In table-oriented terminology it combines rows of tables creating a table with long rows containing parts of all joined tables in the sense described above.

There is not much need for join operations as described above because they combine tuples of different relations which have different keys. Typically, a query relating to a join involves a selection operation on the result of the Cartesian product. We first form the Cartesian product, then we select tuples given by some condition (this condition will be denoted theta here). To simplify this, we define a theta-join operation. The theta-join is a binary operation that allows us to combine the selection and Cartesian product into one operation. The theta-join operator (the arithmetic comparison operator) forms the Cartesian product of its two arguments and then performs a selection using the predicate theta. If the condition theta is =, the operation is then called equi-join. It frequently occurs in practice that theta-join forces equality on those attributes that appear in both relations, i.e. on common attributes. To solve this task the natural join operation has been defined (Fig. 1.16).

Example

We have two tables with information about equipment. Each row describes a piece of equipment. In the first table we have technical parameters such as performance; in the second table we have economic parameters such as price. It would make no sense to perform a join on these tables because this would combine all technical parameters of the piece of equipment E1 with all economic parameters of the piece of equipment E2. On the other hand, it is very useful to do an equi-join with equality of keys, assuming that both tables have the same key identifying the equipment and that the same key value in each table denotes the same piece of equipment.

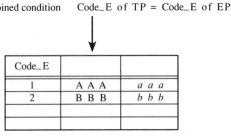

Figure 1.16 Equi-join

Relations are sets of tuples, which means that all set operations, such as union, difference and intersection, can be applied to them (Fig. 1.17).

There are some other operations that could be mentioned but the operations given above are the basic ones and constitute a complete set of operations (assignment, selection, projection, join, union, difference). It can be proved that all other operations can be derived from these.

Finally, it should be shown how to navigate among tables representing relations. This will be done by utilizing the mechanism of primary keys and foreign keys.

As described above, in every table we have columns containing values that uniquely identify rows. Such columns are called primary keys. In the other columns of such a table we can have values which may be used as primary keys in other tables (or in the same table as shown in Fig. 1.18). Such columns are called foreign keys. This is how connections among two or more tables can be expressed (Fig. 1.19 on page 22).

In dBASE-like systems we can express this connection by the statements Set relation to and Set skip to (Fig. 1.20 on page 23).

Originally, the relational model was presented as a set of features. In 1969 the mathematician E.F. Codd developed the theory of the relational model. As shown above, this model is based on set theory and first-order predicate logic. Codd published a standard for implementation known as the twelve Fidelity rules, although there are thirteen of them (they start with rule 0). So far, no commercial database system exists that fulfils all these rules completely without exceptions.

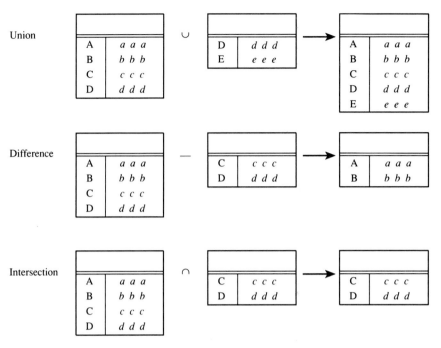

Figure 1.17 Set operations with relations

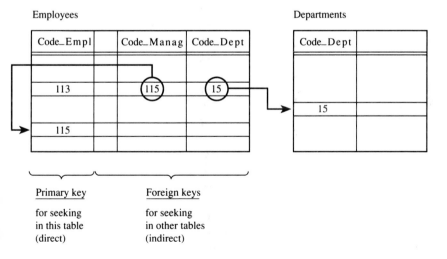

Figure 1.18 Primary keys and foreign keys

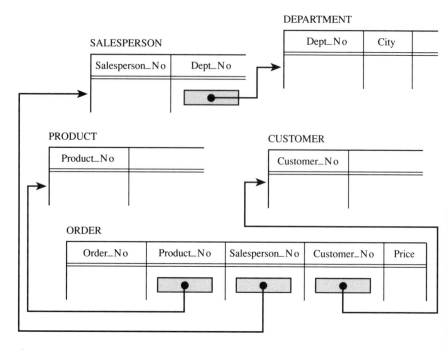

Figure 1.19 Navigation in relational model

There are certainly many reasons for the popularity of the relational model:

- It supports powerful, simple and declarative query languages.
- The results of query operations on relations are themselves relations, so queries can be nested.
- It is very transparent for simple problems.
- There are cheap implementations of database systems based on the relational model for inexpensive home and personal computers.

At this point it is worth noting again that, although the motivation for the relational model was different, it provides a very suitable solution from the point of view of abstract data types. We have an encapsulated module which exports only one type `Table` (this abstract type is para-meterized in the sense of specifying type, size, and number of columns) and we have six methods, i.e. six basic operations on tables. In the terminology of the programming language Ada we can speak of a generic package `Tables-only`, in the terminology of object-oriented programming (Chapter 5) we can speak of a class `Tables-only`.

Shortcomings and weak points of relational databases (including normalization, efficiency, etc.) will be discussed further in Chapter 2.

```
SELECT      1
USE         PRODUCTS
SELECT      2
USE         ORDERS
SET         RELATION TO Code_P INTO PRODUCTS
```

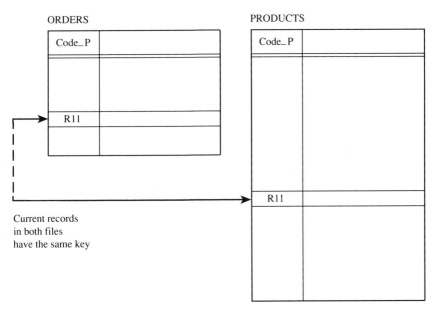

ORDERS

PRODUCTS

Current records
in both files
have the same key

Figure 1.20 Navigation in dBASE-like languages

1.6 THE POINTER-ORIENTED IMPLEMENTATION AND THE NETWORK MODEL

As given above, the implementation of relationships with tables in the relational model is not the only possibility. Another is to represent relationships by pointer parts in the records implementing instances of entities (Fig. 1.21). Note that the first databases were implemented in this way.

If we consider again the problem in Fig. 1.8, at first sight there are the following problems:

- When designing the database we must be sure that it will never be necessary for any teacher to teach more than three subjects. The number of pointers in the pointer part of each record is fixed at the time of design.
- When we use pointers in Teacher-records only it will be very easy and efficient to find an answer to the query: 'What subjects does Mr Brown

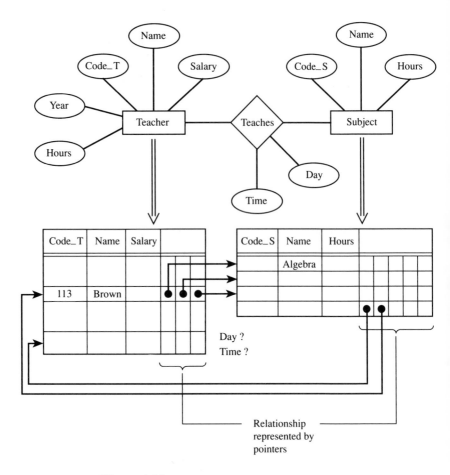

Figure 1.21 Relationship implemented with pointers

teach?' but it could be time consuming to answer an 'inverse' query: 'Who teaches algebra?' In this case, we must search in the table `Teacher` in all pointers of all rows. It follows that we can have predefined paths for some queries which enable efficient processing of these presumed queries. Unfortunately, we cannot install pointers for all possible queries because of the size of the database.

- If we implement our database in this simple way, there is no place to write values of the attribute `Time`, which is an attribute of the relationship `Teaches`.
- Each entity set can take part in many relationships and, in our implementation, we must have one pointer part for each of these relationships.
- Using pointers we can easily implement a binary relationship, i.e. a

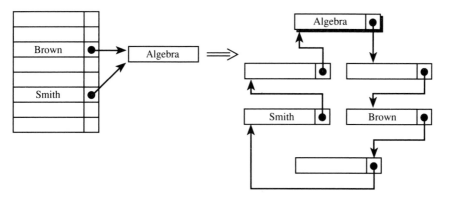

Figure 1.22 A set as a many-to-one relationship

relationship between two entity sets, but when the parity of the implemented relationship is higher, then we must use more sophisticated methods.

These problems led to the introduction of the network data model. We obtain this from the E–R model with all relationships restricted to:

- Binary relationships (this allows us to use pointers)
- Many-to-one relationships (this allows us to use only one pointer for each relationship).

One-to-one relationships are a special case of the many-to-one relationship, so we will only consider many-to-one relationships. Of course, we cannot escape the nature of the model or ignore its inconvenient features. What we lose in implementation by introducing restrictions to the model we must solve on the level of logical design.

Now let us consider the representation of many-to-one relationships. Such a relationship is called a set in the network model (Fig. 1.22). It has its owner (one) and its members (many).

A set can be implemented as a ring data structure with the owner at the head of the chain and with the last member pointing to the owner. Other structures such as bidirectional chains or pointer arrays are often used. Members often have special links to their owner. They can be ordered according to a variety of criteria. As mentioned earlier, the network data model cannot be used to represent three-way or higher-order relationships directly.

This problem will be solved by creating a special link record type containing only pointers to related instances of entities and values of attributes of the relationship (Fig. 1.23).

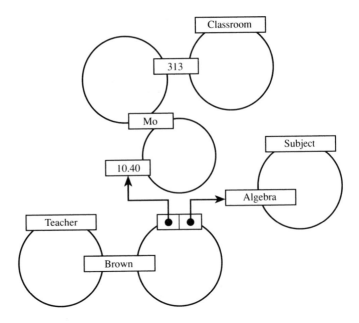

Figure 1.23 Representation of relationship of higher arity

Summarizing, we can say that creating sets enables:

- A member of one set to be the owner of another set
- A member of one set to be a member of another set.

Of course, a member must have at least one pointer field for each set where it is a member. This mechanism will be used to represent many-to-many relationships (Fig. 1.24).

Another pointer-oriented model that could be described is the hierarchical model. This was the first database model used, but we can define it as a subset of the network model for the purposes of this book. It will not be considered here.

We described the network model from the curious programmer's point of view. There is another point of view – that of a database designer at the conceptual level. Since this is not necessary for Chapter 2 we will omit it. As far as the mathematician's point of view is concerned, there is no underlying mathematical theory used here.

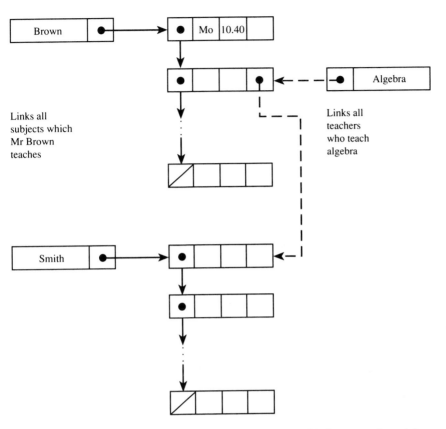

Figure 1.24 Implementation of a many-to-many relationship in a network model

1.7 PROCEDURAL AND DECLARATIVE QUERYING

There are two ways of describing the query:

- Procedural—we need to describe how to obtain the result, i.e. which procedures in which order have to be called.
- Descriptive—we describe only properties of that which we are looking up and the sequence of procedure calls will be generated automatically by the system.

Procedural querying will be used for network databases, descriptive querying for relational databases, represented by SQL.

1.8 DECLARATIVE QUERYING WITH SQL

In Sec. 1.2 we introduced the main idea of a DBMS with the DDL, DML, and DCL languages. In this section we will show the main features of the SQL language, which is based on the relational model. This is now a standard query language for relational databases. It will be used very often, it is very transparent, and we will utilize it in examples as much as possible. It can be used to query the database systems dBASE IV, INGRES, Informix, ORACLE, DB2 and others.

The DDL language includes statements for the definitions of the data structures used in the database. From DDL we will show here only the statement `create table`.

In this section we will use the simple database described using the E–R model in Sec. 1.3.2.

```
Teacher(Code_T, Name, Salary)
Teaches(Code_T, Code_S, Day, Time)
Subject(Code_S, Name)
```

A table can be created using a statement:

```
CREATE TABLE Name (<list of columns definitions>)
```

In the list of columns we must specify their names, types and sizes and constraints if we wish to go into it. Assignment will be done using the statement `insert` from the DML part of SQL:

```
INSERT INTO Name (<list of columns>)
           VALUES (<list of values>)
```

Example
```
CREATE TABLE Teacher (Code_T NUM(3),
                      Name   CHAR(20),
                      Salary NUM(5));

INSERT INTO Teacher (Code_T, Name, Salary)
            VALUES  (113,    "Brown", 2000);
```

The DML language of a DBMS built on the relational model must mirror the basic operations with relations as mentioned in Sec. 1.6. The fundamental operation in SQL is the construct represented syntactically as a `select . . . from . . . where` block.

```
SELECT   <list of columns projected>
FROM     <list of joined tables>
WHERE    <conditions for selection>
```

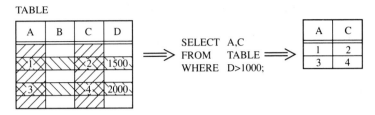

Figure 1.25 Selection and projection in SQL

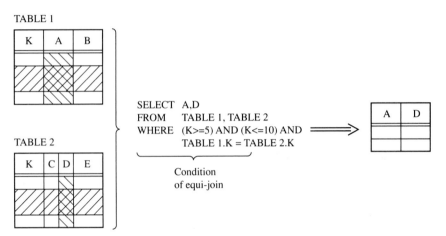

Figure 1.26 Join in SQL

In this statement the operations selection, projection and join can be combined. Our first example uses a single table in the `from`-clause.

A simple selection and projection is shown in Fig. 1.25. The next example in Fig. 1.26 shows how a join is expressed in SQL.

Table names can be used as qualifiers in the `select` and `from` clause to resolve ambiguities (if necessary or for clarity). When a table is evaluated by a query a pointer traverses the table row by row, indicating which row is currently being evaluated for inclusion in the query's output.

By joining a table with itself we can obtain two independent pointers in the same table. It works as if we had two tables with the same contents (Fig. 1.27).

Example

```
Query: Retrieve all employees living in the same town
       as the manager of the department they work
       for.
```

We use one pointer in the table `Employee` for searching employees and their cities, and the second pointer for searching their managers.

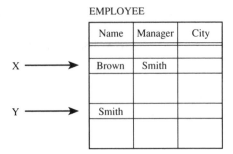

Figure 1.27 A join of a table with itself

```
SELECT    Name
FROM      Employee X, Employee Y
WHERE     X.City = Y.City and X.Manager = Y.Name
```

The set found as an answer can be displayed in an order which is to be specified by an order by-clause in the select . . . from . . . where statement.

Example
```
Query: Display all teachers ordered according to
       their salaries (descending).
    SELECT    Name
    FROM      Teacher
    ORDER BY Salary DESC;
```

Using a group-clause, we can group rows of a table together that have the same value in a given column. When testing properties of such a group we use a having-clause.

Example
```
Query: Retrieve the average salary of teacher groups
       of the same age. Groups with fewer than 4
       members will not be considered.

       SELECT    AVG(Salary)
       FROM      Teacher
       GROUP BY Year
       HAVING    COUNT(Year) > 3;
```

As shown above, the result of a query on a relation is also a relation.

This fact is used in SQL to derive the concept of a subquery. A sub-query is a `select . . . from . . . where` statement which delivers an intermediate result used directly in the 'enclosing' query. A subquery can deliver:

- A single value
- A row (i.e. a tuple)
- A column (i.e. a set of single values)
- A table (i.e. a set of tuples)

The first two cases can be written simply because SQL can compare tuples in the same way as single values.

Example

```
Query:  Retrieve all employees having the same type of
        car as Mr Brown.
        SELECT    Name
        FROM      Employee
        WHERE     Car=
                  (SELECT   Car
                   FROM     Employee
                   WHERE    Name = "Brown");
Query:  Retrieve all employees having the same type of
        car including the year of production as Mr
        Brown.
        SELECT    Name
        FROM      Employee
        WHERE     (Car, Year)=
                  (SELECT   Car, Year
                   FROM     Employee
                   WHERE    Name= "Brown");
```

When the result of a subquery is a set we can use the following oper-ators: `in`, `any`, `all`, and `exists`. The `in` operator represents the mem-bership operator, i.e. it tests whether the left-hand operand is a member of the set given as the right-hand operand.

Example

```
Query:  Retrieve all employees whose manager is a
        Spanish native speaker.
        SELECT    Name
        FROM      Employee
        WHERE     Manager IN
                  (SELECT   Name
                   FROM     Manager
```

```
                    WHERE      Language = "Spanish");
```
The exists operator provides a test of whether the set produced is empty.

Example

```
Query: Retrieve names of teachers teaching algebra.
           SELECT   Name
           FROM     Teacher
           WHERE    EXISTS
                    (SELECT    Code_T
                     FROM      Teaches
                     WHERE     Teacher.Code_T=
                               Teaches.Code_T
                                   AND Code_S =
                    (SELECT    Code_S
                     FROM      Subject
                     WHERE     Name = "algebra")
                    );
```

To express quantifiers we have the operators any and all. These operators must be used together with comparison operators, as both of them compare single values to the sets of values returned by the subquery.

The operator any is interpreted as follows. The condition, namely, f<operator> any {set S} evaluates to true if and only if the value f fulfils the condition given by the operator in combination with at least one value in the set S. The intuitive interpretation (in the sense that it would normally be understood in English) is misleading. Any has been used in send of some, i.e. some member of the set makes the comparison true. The comparison = any is identical to the use of the operator in. The operator all is interpreted as follows: The condition f <operator> all {set S} evaluates to true if and only if the value f fulfils the given conditions for all values in the set S.

Example

```
Query: Find all teachers from the Department of Math-
       ematics who teach more hours than any teacher
       from the Department of Physics.
       SELECT   Name
       FROM     Teacher
       WHERE    Hours
                ALL (SELECT   Hours
                     FROM     Teacher
                     WHERE    Dept = "Physics")
                        AND   Dept = "Mathematics"
       ORDER BY Hours DESC;
```

As mentioned in Sec. 1.6, we need to represent set operations because they belong to the basic operations. We use operators union and intersect in the following way.

Example

Query: Which teachers are either teaching algebra or
       doing research in algebra?

```
       SELECT    Name
       FROM      Teaches
       WHERE     Teaches.Code_S =
                 (SELECT    Subject.Code_S
                  FROM      Subject
                  WHERE     Name = "algebra")
       UNION
       SELECT    Name
       FROM      Teacher
       WHERE     Research = "algebra"
```

There are built-in functions that can be used to compute properties of sets (columns). We have:

- Count: number of values
- Sum: sum of the values
- Avg: average of the values
- Max: largest value
- Min: smallest value.

There are many good books (e.g. Date, 1989; Date and White, 1989) giving a complete description of the SQL language. The brief overview outlined above will be sufficient for our examples in the following chapters and for comparison with object-oriented features.

Before leaving this topic we will stress the simplicity (queries are expressed very concisely), completeness and non-procedurality of SQL. From relational algebra we know that we can express all queries based on the relational model by using the given constructs. All queries are expressed in a descriptive, non-procedural way, i.e. we specify what result we need without saying how the result should be obtained.

1.9 SPEEDING UP PROCESSING

Simple methods such as sequential searching in a table cannot be used for large bodies of data because it would be too time consuming. For the same reason, we cannot process a complex query from left to right exactly as

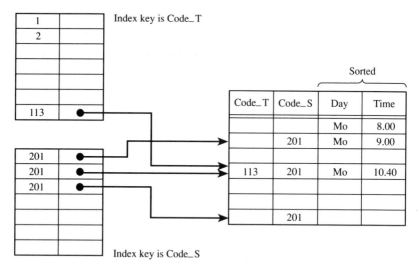

Figure 1.28 Indexing files

written. We use indexing methods for searching in tables and files and query optimization methods for query processing.

1.9.1 Indexing

It is known from the theory that we can search in a table quickly when the table is sorted, and we can use an appropriate method such as binary search. Each table can be sorted only in one way, i.e. in an order for one key. When we need to search by attribute A in a table sorted by attribute B we can only write the new order of the rows by the attribute B into some new table. A table made in this way is called an index table (Fig. 1.28) and it contains two columns. In the first column there are ordered values of the chosen attribute, and in the second column there are order numbers (or addresses) of the rows of the table. In simple database systems where each row will be implemented as a record of a file we can find there the numbers of records which, combined with the address of the beginning of the file, allow us to compute the disk address of each record. Very often more sophisticated methods of indexing will be used (e.g. B-trees).

1.9.2 Query optimization

In simple database systems the user must say what index table (i.e. what index file) should be used. In advanced database systems it will be implicitly decided by the system. This is part of the process called query optimization. It is the problem not only of using suitable indexing tables but also of the order in which the parts of the query should take part in processing.

Besides primary and foreign keys, there are also secondary keys. A secondary key is a data item that does not uniquely identify a row in a table but identifies a number of records in a set that share the same property.

Example
Query: How many teachers are 40 years old?

1. Solution: We search sequentially in the table and count all rows where in the item AGE is 40.
2. Solution: We use the item AGE as a secondary key and therefore we have an index table having in the first column all values of AGE and in the second column sets of teacher's names.

As shown above, we prepare secondary index tables when assuming queries which can effectively use them. We can group together all rows of a table having a common property, and in this way create a so-called inverted list structure. When we do this using all of the columns, we get an inverted file.

Some relational DBMSs use clever schemes to reduce the cost of using indexes. Each query to be processed is modified into a special form. This disjunctive normal form (DNF) restructures the where clauses of a query into a set of conjunctions with only OR operators between conjunctions and only AND and NOT operators within conjunctions. Any query can be translated into DNF.

Example
WHERE (Age> 50 or Age< 30) and (Language = "Spanish")

can be written into DNF as

WHERE (Age > 50 and Language = "Spanish") or
      (Age < 30 and Language = "Spanish")

In this scheme we use the fact that the AND operator causes items from two inverted lists to be intersected and the OR operator causes items from two inverted lists to be merged.

Indexes appear to be the data structures chosen for relational databases because of the similarity of Boolean select . . . where clauses to inverted list intersection and merger. Manipulating index entries is like manipulating the tuples to which the entries point. Trying to determine an efficient pointer sequential network path for a query would cause a lot of overhead. Fast response, at the expense of extra index space, seems to be the popular choice.

1.10 CONCURRENCY IN DATABASES

Computers are not mathematical objects but electronic equipment, and sometimes it happens that there is a failure in hardware (e.g. loss of power, disk head crash) or in software which leads to a system crash. We can distinguish between a system failure (main memory contents lost) and a media failure (disk memory contents lost). If operators are running programs for solving an equation, they can simply start them again, but if they are running a data processing task they could obtain inconsistent data, which is not acceptable.

Let us use the following example. In a bank there is a sum of money (e.g. 100) that should be transferred from account A1 to account A2.

```
read (A1)
A1 := A1 - 100
write (A1)
read (A2)
A2 := A2 + 100
write (A2)
```

This is a very simple program but a failure can cause account A1 to be less than it was at the beginning (100 was subtracted) while leaving account A2 the same as at the beginning, because the failure came before account A2 was modified on the disk.

Note here that in the program given above we cannot see when the I/O operations will be performed. It can all be run completely or partially in buffers.

The solution is in a mechanism called transaction management. A transaction is a sequence of operations which must be performed completely. It may not be terminated abnormally. We say that a transaction must be atomic (i.e. it occurs either in its entirety or not at all). In processing a transaction we want the change to the database to be made only if the transaction in its entirety is processed successfully. Since we cannot guarantee this, each transaction will be performed first on a so-called log file, and then committed if successful or performed again if unsuccessful. The only way to recover from a media failure is to have a backup copy of the database that is up to date at all times. The most common tool for protecting against loss of data when a system failure occurs is a log or journal which contains the history of all changes made to the database and the status of each transaction.

If the transaction fails at any point, we say that it has aborted and we do not want any of the changes to be made. To maintain transaction integrity, the DBMS must provide facilities for the user or application programmer to define transaction boundaries—that is, the logical beginning and end of transactions. The DBMS should then commit changes for successful transactions and reject changes for aborted ones. The DBMS must be able to restore the database in the event of system failure. This will be achieved by logging, i.e. by using the log file. In many systems, we can use the statement rollback explicitly.

Example

In dBASE we can use statements on error rollback and set reprocess. They will try to perform the transaction repeatedly (in the following example 15 times).

```
SET REPROCESS TO 15
ON ERROR ROLLBACK
BEGIN TRANSACTION
REPLACE ALL A WITH A * 1.08
END TRANSACTION
ON ERROR
```

We described the problem of transaction management in the simplest possible form, i.e. as a recovery from crashes in a single-user environment. In a multi-user environment we must not only solve possible effects of failures but also consider concurrently running transactions in time-sharing systems (or in multi-processor systems) on shared data.

To manage concurrency, the database must be partitioned into items, which are units of data to which access is controlled. The size of the items used by a system is often called its granularity. The most common way to control access to items is through locking. A lock manager is the part of a DBMS that controls access privileges to a single item (this item can be a row or a table in the relational DBMS). These privileges can be granted or withheld from a transaction. The following kinds of locks are common:

- Locks providing shared access (the locked item is accessible to all transactions but only for reading).
- Locks providing exclusive access (the locked item is accessible only to the privileged transaction).

In the first part of this section we introduced transaction management as a tool for protecting the consistency of data. Now we can introduce locking (which is a part of transaction management) as a mechanism for protecting transactions from interference from other, concurrently executing transactions – i.e. the presence of one transaction in the system should not cause another transaction to produce incorrect results. The purpose of the lock is basically to guarantee that no other transaction can update the locked item, i.e. if transaction T1 can update the item, then no other transaction T2 can destroy that update by overwriting it. The rule is that a transaction must hold a lock on an item in order to be able to update that item. If transaction T1 updates an item, then concurrent transactions will not be allowed to also update this item until the lock is released. Any concurrent transaction attempting to access such an item will have to wait until the transaction holding the lock reaches its end-of-transaction statement.

In the simple approach the lock manager, which is a part of a transaction manager, works on a table which consists of tuples (<*locked item*>, <*type of lock*>, <*transaction*>). The locked item is the key in this table. The lock manager provides the following operations:

- To find locks on a given item.
- To find locks when a transaction begins.
- To find locks when a transaction ends.

The operation of locking acts as a synchronization tool. In every concurrent system synchronized in this way there is a danger of the situation called 'deadlock'. This could arise if a transaction T1 needs to lock the items A and B, and a transaction T2 needs to lock the items B and A. First, transaction T1 locks A, and transaction T2 simultaneously locks B, then T2 cannot run and is waiting for transaction T1 to release the lock on item A. Since each transaction is waiting, it cannot unlock the item the other transaction needs to proceed. They would wait for ever.

A simple strategy for preventing deadlock is as follows. Each transaction requests all its locks at once and tells the lock manager to grant them all, if possible, or to grant none and make the process wait, which would happen if one or more locks are held by another transaction. The other possible strategy is to order the items and require all transactions to request locks in the same order. Then we will have a first-come-first-served strategy. The second possibility is not to prevent deadlocks but to periodically test the lock requests. If a deadlock is discovered (using waits-for graphs), at least one of the deadlocked transactions must be restarted. Its effects on the database may not be committed until it is successful.

1.11 DISTRIBUTED DATABASES

In the previous sections we assumed that all data is stored at one place, as shown in Fig. 1.3. We can imagine a bank which has its central office

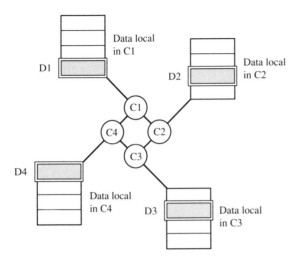

Figure 1.29 The main idea of distributed databases

and branch offices (perhaps in other cities or countries). It would be possible, of course, to connect all branch offices with the central office via the communications network and to work in the way described above but it would be very expensive. The main idea of distributed databases is shown in Fig. 1.29. The database is not stored in its entirety at a single physical location but rather is spread across a network of computers that are geographically dispersed and connected via communications links. It is important that data is stored at the location where it is most frequently used (often where it is created), but is still available to users at other locations.

Data distribution has advantages: it combines the efficiency of local processing (no communications overheads) with all the advantages provided by a centralized database system. There are also disadvantages. The communications overheads may be high, and there are also significant technical difficulties in implementing such a system.

This should not affect users. They should not normally need to know at which location any given piece of data is physically stored. From the programmer's point of view there are many interesting problems, e.g. how to keep the database system operational when a link (i.e. a connection line) or a node (i.e. a computer in the net) is out of order. The solution, to keep copies of data in different nodes, brings again an interesting problem of updating these copies. We will discuss these problems in more detail in Chapter 12. For a better understanding, we can recommend the book Ceri *et al.* (1984).

In the previous sections a brief introduction to database technology was given. There are good books (of around 500 to 1000 pages) covering this introduction (e.g. Date, 1986; El Masri and Navathe, 1989; Korth and Silberschatz, 1986; Ullman, 1982, 1988; Wiederhold, 1986) and if you have enough time we recommend that you read at least one of them.

TWO
SHORTCOMINGS OF THE RELATIONAL MODEL

In Chapter 1 we showed the advantages of relational database systems. In this chapter, we will describe the shortcomings of relational database systems which led to the development of object-oriented systems.

2.1 PROBLEMS OF SPLITTING COMPLEX OBJECTS

In Sec. 1.6 we mentioned a condition whereby attributes of entities which must be fulfilled due to the relational model could be used. This condition requires that domains of attributes can contain only single values in the sense that these values may not have any internal structure (they must be atomic), i.e. we cannot work with a domain of lists, tuples, etc.

In practice, it means that if it is possible to represent each object in the database (i.e. each instance of each entity) by a single row in a table representing a relation whose attributes have only atomic values, then we have a very simple model and we can be sure of obtaining a very efficient implementation. If a domain of at least one attribute is a set of objects which have an internal structure such as lists, tuples, etc. then we must start a process called normalization of relations, which causes splitting attributes of one object into more than one table.

2.1.1 Normalization and decomposition

A relation whose attributes domains are sets of atomic values (type: integer, real, Boolean, character, date, string) is called a relation in the first normal form (1. NF). Now we will discuss the problem of what to do when

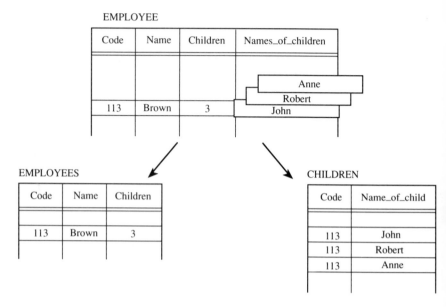

Figure 2.1 A three-dimensional table and its decomposition

the reality which is modelled contains domains with structured values.

Example
Figure 2.1 shows a table Employee which is obviously not in the 1. NF.
Data about any children is a part of an employee's record.

As we can see in Fig. 2.1, the domain of the attribute Names-of-
Children contains lists of different lengths as its elements and the relation Employee is therefore not in the 1. NF.

To obtain relations in the 1. NF we must split the given relation into
more relations. This process is called decomposition. Each new relation
constructed during the decomposition must contain the key of the original
relation. We obtain one relation by projection of the former relation on
the columns which have domains with atomic values, and then we have
one relation for each domain with structured values. These relations are
created from the keys and the values stored in the structures of their
domains. Relations in the 1. NF are called flat relations.

The problem of structured values in domains is not the only one. In
Fig. 2.2 we have a simple table with some semantic information which is
called functional dependencies. We know that Price depends on the
tuple <*Supplier, Product*>, and we use it as a key in this table. On the
other hand, we know that the customs-duty depends only on the product.
It partially depends on only part of the complete key. These facts result
from the semantics of the real world.

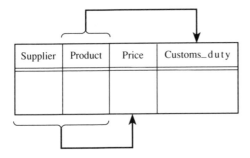

Figure 2.2 A functional dependency on a subset of a key

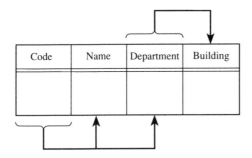

Figure 2.3 A functional dependency between secondary keys

Another case of functional dependency is shown in Fig. 2.3. There we see that the attribute Building does not depend on the key directly but transitively, i.e. *Code→Department→Building*. The properties of the tables shown in Figs. 2.2 and 2.3 introduce the following problems:

- Insertion anomaly
- Deletion anomaly
- Update anomaly.

Insertion anomaly means that we can insert only a complete row into the table. If we found, for example, Product and Customs-duty we cannot insert this information into the table Products, because we do not know the Supplier, which is part of the key. We cannot insert a row into a table when we do not know its key, i.e. when we do not know its position in the table.

Deletion anomaly can be illustrated using Fig. 2.3. If the last teacher of a department were to be fired, we would lose the information about the location of the department.

Update anomaly is caused by the redundancy in Fig. 2.3. If a department has 100 teachers, then in each case we repeat the information about the location of the department. If the department changes its building, or

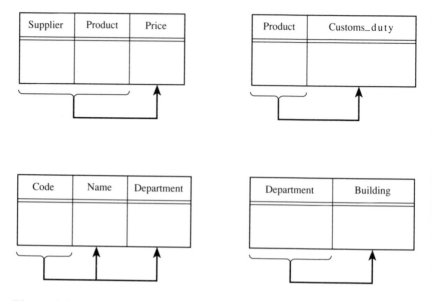

Figure 2.4 Relations without partial dependencies and without transitive dependencies

if the building changes its name, we must update many items. The solution to these problems is again in decomposition. We split the tables as shown in Fig. 2.4.

We described reasons for splitting an entity description from one table into several, and we note that the idea presented in Chapter 1—that every instance of every entity (i.e. every object of the real world) should be represented by one row in one table—can no longer be followed.

In fact, the reason of normal forms derived from the functional dependencies (2. NF and 3. NF) is that more than one entity was represented by the split relation. In other words, our estimation of what an entity is was not correct. As written in Alagić (1986): 'Normal forms are formal rules for determining whether or not a relation represents a single entity.'

Using normalization we can transform our primary model to another model with another system of entities which can be represented as a system of two-dimensional tables.

Example

The priority demand in classrooms is necessary for somebody who is teaching LISP and needs a classroom with LISP-machines (Fig. 2.5).

The table shown in Fig. 2.5 has been split (i.e. decomposed) into four tables, but, in many cases, we can get many hundreds of 3. NF tables for one table representing a non-first normal form relation.

Table of courses								
Course_no	Dept.	Subject	Type	Person	Students in the past		Room demanded	
					Period	Students	Classroom	Priority
213	Math	Algebra	Lect	Brown	1 . Q . 85	100	A 115	1
					3 . Q . 85	40	B 100	5
					1 . Q . 86	150	A 115	1
					3 . Q . 86	40	B 100	5
214	Math	Algebra	Exc	Smith				

LECTURES

Course_no	Dept.	Subject	Type
213	Math	Algebra	Lect

HISTORY

Teacher	Course_no	Period	Students

TEACHERS

Person	Course_no
Brown	213
Brown	512

ROOMS

Classroom	Course_no	Period	Priority

Figure 2.5 A decomposition

Example
In CAD databases we can represent three-dimensional objects in the following way. Each object will be decomposed into a combination (supported
by set operations) of transformed primitive basic objects (Fig. 2.6).

It is not difficult to imagine a description of a relatively simple part
which would be dispersed in some hundred tables. This phenomenon is
very useful when we need to process one property of all instances of one
entity in the normalized model, but it is a burden when we need to process
all properties of one whole object, i.e. one complete instance of an entity
in the real-world model.

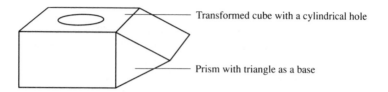

OBJECTS

Code_O	Description
Obj1	Hammer

PARTS

Code_P	Code_O	Type
P1	Obj1	Primitive
P101	Obj1	Combined
P102	Obj1	Transformed_by_scaling
P103	Obj1	Transformed_by_shifting

TRANSFORMED_PARTS_BY_SHIFTING

Code_P	Code_primitive	Param

TRANSFORMED_PARTS_BY_SCALING

Code_P	

COMBINED_PARTS

CUBES

CYLINDERS

PRIMITIVE_PARTS

Code_primitive	Type
P1	Cube
P2	Cylinder
P3	Prism

PRISMS

Figure 2.6 A picture in a database

Example
Let us imagine a model of a relational database for a store of Christmas trees. Each Christmas tree will be decomposed into stem, branches, and needles. Each part of the tree will have the tree identifier as one of its properties (as a part of a key). Then we put all stems in a Stem-box, all branches in a Branch-box and all needles in a Needle-box.

This organization is very suitable if we have to answer 'How many 5-inch branches do we have in our store altogether?' but it is not suitable for selling complete Christmas trees. If someone wishes to buy a Christmas tree then we must go through all the boxes and look up parts with the same Stem-key as the stem selected by the customer.

The problem is how to obtain a description of a whole complex object from the database when necessary. The structure of the whole object is not stored directly in the data dictionary of the database. In the data dictionary of a relational database there can be found everything about all the stored tables (representing relations) and their columns (representing attributes), but there is nothing stored about how to collect all properties of an object from the real world. In the data dictionary the primary real-world model with its complex objects having structured attribute values is not stored, but what is stored is the secondary normalized model, which was derived using the normalization process. We can describe this problem as one of modelling power.

The information about reassembling objects from tables is stored indirectly in procedures which must be called up to obtain a complex object together from different tables. Running these procedures can be time consuming and it often causes problems with performance.

2.2 PROBLEMS OF OBJECT SYNTHESIS

There are two ways to collect the description of an object, i.e. all attributes of an object, from many tables:

- A synthesis using join operations
- A synthesis using navigation through foreign keys.

In the first approach we follow relational algebra, where the join operation is used for this purpose. As shown in Sec. 1.6, the join operation is a subset of the Cartesian product. This is a very time-consuming operation. In the second approach we give the programmer the responsibility for writing the correct logical operations for all tables, which will be accessed or connected by pointers.

The first approach is used in databases systems based on SQL, the second in database systems based on dBASE-like languages. We will describe both of these briefly in the following subsections.

2.2.1 An SQL-synthesis of an object

When using SQL in its pure form we have no other tool for synthesis of an object description than the join operation.

```
SELECT    <list of all object properties>
FROM      <list of tables where the properties are
          stored>
WHERE     <conditions of the joins>
```

We must emphasize again that the list of tables where the properties of the object are stored is not stored in the data dictionary but must be given in the clause from in the SQL query statement.

Example

To synthesize object No. 177 in the Christmas tree database:

```
SELECT    STEM_BOX.*, BRANCH_BOX.*, NEEDLE_BOX.*
FROM      STEM_BOX, BRANCH_BOX, NEEDLE_BOX
WHERE     STEM_BOX.STEM_KEY   = 177
     AND  BRANCH_BOX.STEM_KEY = 177
     AND  NEEDLE_BOX.STEM_KEY = 177
```

This will often be an equi-join operation but not always. There are many clever optimizing techniques but the complexity of the join operation is still considerable.

When using SQL in embedded mode (Chapter 3) we can simulate the navigation through foreign keys described in the following subsection.

2.2.2 A dBASE-synthesis of an object

Database systems using a dBASE-language began with dBASE II on small computers under CP/M without a hard disk. In principle, it was not possible to use a join operation. In the set of operations of dBASE one can find a join statement, but its purpose is to create a new table (i.e. a new file) containing desired data. If one uses it for large tables it will probably run all night.

For composing an object with parts from many tables (better to say, for accessing an object's parts stored in many tables) there is the set relation to statement. Note that each table in dBASE is represented by a file, and that we can use altogether 10 working areas in the main memory for 10 opened data files. We will describe some properties of the statement set relation to for the purpose of illustrating navigation in the relational model. The main idea is that we have some tables stored in working areas, and for each table there is a pointer at the current row. Using set relation to, we describe the logical connection under tables for the purpose of collecting properties of the given object. We obtain a chain of tables. This chain of tables can be considered here as a representation of the whole object structure. If we set the pointer of the first table in the chain on the key value identifying the given object, the statement set relation to provides the movement of all pointers in the chained tables to rows representing properties of the given object. For connected columns of tables, we must have index tables.

Example

Query: For each COURSE we need to know: Who is teach-
       ing it now, how many students came to the
       teacher's lectures in the past, which class-
       room had to be reserved.

```
SELECT    1
USE       LECTURES
SELECT    2
USE       TEACHERS
SELECT    3
USE       HISTORY
SELECT    4
USE       ROOMS


SELECT    1
SET RELATION TO CourseNo INTO TEACHERS
SELECT    2
SET RELATION TO Teacher INTO HISTORY
SELECT  3
SET RELATION TO CourseNo + Period INTO ROOMS
```

Pointers A, B, C, D are now set to logically connected rows describing properties of one object (Fig. 2.7).

This method seems to be better in performance but:

• Complete responsibility is transferred to the programmer who has to write all connections and logical operations.
• It was probably never tested for major tasks because of limitations concerning the number of opened files, used working areas, etc.

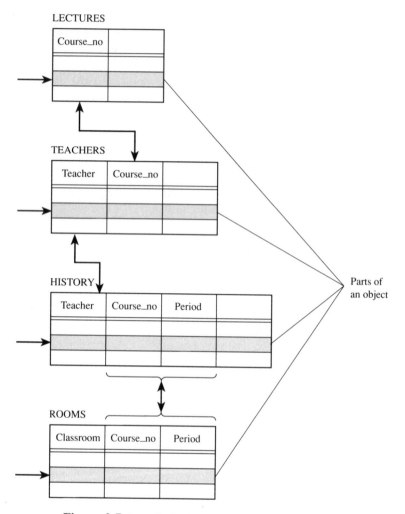

Figure 2.7 A synthesis of an object in dBASE languages

At this point, note that in the dBASE family we can include the Clipper database system which offers 255 working areas for this purpose. In each there can be one data file and 15 index files opened. Each datafile in each working area can be connected by a `set relation to` statement to eight other data files.

2.3 PROBLEMS OF RECURSIVE QUERYING

In Sec. 2.2 we described how to obtain a flat tuples description of complex objects and a complex object from flat tuples. Another problem is in

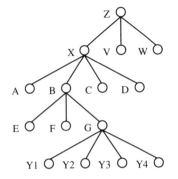

Name	List of direct subordinates
Z	{X, V, W}
X	{A, B, C, D}
B	{E, F, G}
G	{Y1, Y2, Y3, Y4}

Figure 2.8 A hierarchical structure and transitivity

the limitation of traditional query languages. It has been proved that the relational query languages do not allow expression of the computation of the transitive closure of a relation. The transitive closure of a binary relation R is the smallest relation S that includes R and is transitive, that is, $S(X, Y)$ and $S(Y, Z)$ imply $S(X, Z)$.

In the following example we will show a typical application and explain the motivation of transitive closure of queries.

Example

To investigate the hierarchical structure of an office trying to find if Mr Y3 is a subordinate of Mr X (Fig. 2.8) we show the hierarchical structure in Table 2.1. From the table, we see that Mr Y3 is not directly subordinate to Mr X but we must investigate if he is not directly subordinate to any of A, B, C, D, etc. This means that we must investigate if Mr Y3 belongs to a subtree with a root built by Mr X.

Table 2.1

Name	List of direct subordinates
Z	{ X, V, W }
X	{ A, B, C, D }
. . .	
B	{ E, F, G }
. . .	
G	{ Y1, Y2, Y3, Y4 }

We see that the query has to be applied repeatedly and the number of steps is not known previously. In the relational model with underlying relational algebra, i.e. in SQL, tools are not available for writing a loop except for a quantifier. That is why we cannot express this type of query in the relational model.

The problem is, we need to ask them. It was found that more than 15 per cent of all queries to an airport database were of the following kind: 'I am searching the cheapest connection from X to Y. It is not important how many times I will have to change.'

2.4 PROBLEMS OF INEFFICIENCY

As shown above, relational databases have two main shortcomings (Maier, 1989):

- Lack of modelling power
- Lack of performance.

Both of these are created by decomposition. This is why most CAD systems either perform their own data management on top of the operating system's file system or use only some specific services of a relational database system. As discussed in Sec. 1.2, the file processing system concept has disadvantages in not understanding the structure of the data items. This is important for integrity and for storage mapping driven by context. If a CAD system is built atop a relational database, then it uses its operations exclusively for selection, because of the efficient indexing routines, or for projection. Further, features are used which concern recovery, concurrency control and buffer management.

The main reason that the commercial database systems are not fast enough to support today's interactive design tools is that they are built for other tasks. Commercial database systems were developed for use in bank agendas where the actions mostly required are:

- To obtain a few tuples from a relation and update them.
- To select large groups of tuples from a relation and perform the same operation on them.

In the case of bank agendas, the structure of the real-world entities fits very well with the logical (and so far with the physical) structure of the database.

When designing an integrated circuit the situation is quite different. Rerouting a wire can be a process taking up to half an hour because this one change must be propagated to many tables.

Summarizing, we can stress the following main reasons for the unsuitability of commercial relational databases for manipulating structured complex objects:

- Normalization and its requirements for the splitting of complex objects increases the level of indirection between an object and its representation in the normalized relational model. Reassembling the pieces of the description of an object requires many join operations, and it is too time consuming.

- Commercial systems are optimized for high transaction throughput, i.e. for large amounts of simple transactions. Demands of transactions are collected together and the disk accesses, which are to be made for this collection of transactions, are optimized. For CAD systems, a small amount of complex transactions must be processed and a fast response to individual transactions is required. Design transactions can be long-lived, i.e. the designer can continuously work on the update.

There are two possibilities of overcoming these disadvantages:

- To extend the relational model.
- To substitute for the relational DBMS something which represents objects in their entirety within a single data structure because, as we have seen, the splitting (the necessary decomposition) of the representation of an object causes most of the problems. Such a representation is offered by an object-oriented DBMS.

Both possibilities will be discussed (the extensions of the relational model in Chapter 3, the object-oriented approach in the rest of this book).

THREE
EXTENSIONS OF THE RELATIONAL MODEL

As shown in Chapter 2, there are some shortcomings in the use of the relational model. Commercial and experimental database systems problems are resolved by extensions of the pure relational model. The answers to the problem of splitting a complex object are:

- Nested relations
- Surrogates.

The answer to the problem of recursive querying is the embedded mode in SQL.

Further, we will discuss the concept of integrity constraints and the concept of triggers, because it should be stressed that the goal of the development of DBMSs is to store in the data dictionary as much semantic information in descriptive form as possible.

3.1 NESTED RELATIONS

In Sec. 1.6 we introduced a relational algebra on single-valued domains. As shown in Sec. 2.1, properties of real-world objects differ and the solution by decomposition has its shortcomings. It is natural to consider possibilities of a relational algebra that would accept a relation as a value of an attribute.

The idea of the nested relational model is simply to allow relations at any place where attributes occur (Fig. 3.1). Hence, attribute values may either be atomic or relations. This (hierarchical) nesting of relations may be repeated for an arbitrary (but fixed) number of levels.

When defining nested relations where attributes may be relations

Table of departments								
				Teachers				
						Teaches		
Dept_no	Dept_name	Number	Name	Subject no	Subject name	Day	Time	Room
101	Mathematics	62501	Brown	113	Alg	Mo	10.40	3 . 1 . 01
				115	Calc	Tu	9.00	3 . 2 . 01
		42015	Smith					

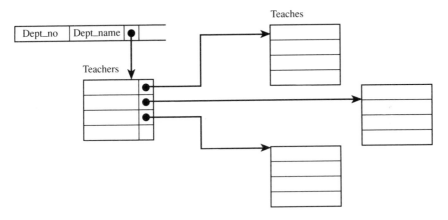

Figure 3.1 Nested relation—level 2

valued, obviously the 'flat' definition becomes recursive. We can speak of a schema of a nested relation, which is a set of attribute descriptions each of which consists of an attribute name and an attribute schema. If an attribute schema is empty as a set, then this attribute is an atomic one, otherwise the schema describes the relations contained in the attribute values. Accordingly, the domain of an attribute is either a set of primitives (for an atomic attribute) or the powerset of the Cartesian product of the domains of the subattributes. Hence, every valid value of a non-atomic attribute is a set of tuples over the corresponding domains, which reflects the idea of 'nested' relations. Schemata of nested relations can be represented by trees and values by nested tables.

A suitable language is necessary for manipulation of nested relations. It should follow a simple idea: whenever a relation is encountered at some place in the language, we wish to allow the application of queries expressed in that language. We will call such a language a nested SQL.

Table of courses								
					Personnel		Room demand	
					History			
Course_no	Dept_name	Course_name	Type	Person	Time	Students	Room	Priority
113	Mathematics	Algebra	Lect	Brown	1 . Q . 85	100	A 115	1
					3 . Q . 85	40	B 100	5
					1 . Q . 86	150	A 115	1
					3 . Q . 86	40	B 100	5
				Smith				

Figure 3.2 Nested relation – level 1

Example

We can describe a nested relation in an SQL-like notation:

```
CREATE TABLE Departments
    (DeptNumber    NUMBER,
    DeptName       CHAR(20),
    (TABLE Teachers
            (TeacherNumber    NUMBER,
            TeacherName       CHAR(25),
            (TABLE Teaches
                (SubjectNumber    NUMBER,
                SubjectName       CHAR(25),
                Day               CHAR(2),
                Time              CHAR(8),
                Room              CHAR(8)
            )
            )
    )
    )
```

We will show how to query and manipulate data in nested relations in the next example and we will use a relation given in Fig. 3.2. This will be defined as:

```
CREATE TABLE Courses (    CourseNo    : NUMBER,
                          DeptName    : CHAR(25),
                          CourseName:   CHAR(25),
                          Type        : CHAR(4),
            (TABLE Personal (    Person     : CHAR(15),
                  (TABLE History(Time        : CHAR(10),
                          Students    : NUMBER
                    )
```

```
              )
                        )
        ),
    (TABLE  RoomDemand( Room        :  CHAR(5),
                        Priority    :  NUMBER
                        )
        )
                        )
```

Before querying, the nested relation must be filled with data:

```
INSERT  INTO  Courses  (CourseNo, DeptName,
                        CourseName,  Type,
        (INSERT  INTO  Personal(Person,
            (INSERT  INTO  History(Time,  Students)),
            (INSERT  INTO  RoomDemand(Room,  Priority))
                        )
)                       )
VALUES  (113,  "Math",  "Algebra",  "Lect",
                ("Brown",("1.Q.85",100),
                ("A115",1))
        )
```

In the insert statement we name all columns, nested tables and their columns which have to be inserted—a list of structures—and then we write a list of values. The structures of the two lists must match.

As shown in Sect. 1.8, the select . . . from . . . where statement is the only querying statement in SQL. We need not express the structure of a nested relation if it is not necessary:

```
SELECT    DeptName,  History
FROM      Courses
```

We can use nested relations in the from-clause in the following way (Fig. 3.3).

Example

```
Query: For each course display teachers who were
       teaching it in the past at the same time, and
       display how many students preferred their lec-
       tures or exercises.
SELECT    CourseNo
       (SELECT P1.Person
(SELECT   P2.Person,  Time,  P1.Students,  P2.Students
```

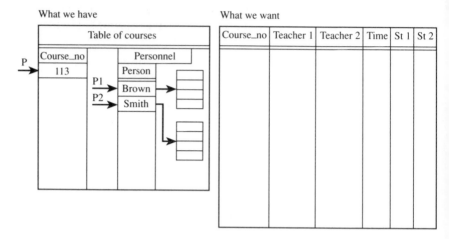

Figure 3.3 A nested query in SQL-like query language

```
FROM      P1.History, Courses.Personal P2
WHERE     P1.Person <> P2.Person
          AND
     P1.History.Time IN (SELECT    P2.History.Time
                         FROM      P2.History
                         )
)
          FROM    Courses.Personal P1)
FROM      Courses;
```

Many nested SQL-like languages have been proposed but there has been no standard until now. We have used only the main idea here without specifying details.

By using nested relations with a nested SQL we solved only one of the shortcomings of the relational model—its lack of modelling power. The additional modelling power made available by nesting allows the representation of a higher-level user interface. At the high level, objects that have set-valued fields can be represented by a single tuple rather than several tuples. The correspondence between a tuple and an entity in the user view leads to a more natural interface.

Nesting is also useful for physical organization of data. At the lower level, implementation techniques such as clustering or repeating fields can be represented using the formalism of the nested relational model. This added power is due to the fact that a nested relation expresses more from the semantics because it includes the structure which cannot be represented in the 1. NF relations.

A difficulty with the use of any relational language within a programming language interface is that typical programming languages are record-oriented while relation languages are set-oriented.

The extension of SQL is a step towards the incorporation of the class-subclass semantics of object-oriented databases into a nested relational framework, as we will explain later. Still lacking in the nested relational model is a means of representing executable code within the data model. Such a representation is used for methods in the object-oriented approach.

3.2 OBJECT IDENTITY AND THE SURROGATE CONCEPT

In the relational model every row of a table will be uniquely identified by a user-defined key which can cause the following problems:

- The key is unique only within the table.
- In different tables, different types and different combinations of attributes are used as keys.
- During development, there may be a requirement that the identification system chosen by the user should be changed (e.g. two companies using a different identification system merge).
- In CAD applications a mouse will be used for manipulation with an interface and it will not be convenient to force the user to identify each part of the constructed equipment.

As a solution, a surrogate will be defined (Fig. 3.4). This is a system-defined and system-generated globally unique identifier for each object in the database. It will not be changed during the lifetime of the object. System date and time are often parts of this identifier. It is persistent and independent of object state or object address. The user has read-only access to it. Using the surrogate, the following extensions can be made:

- Nested relations (Sec. 3.4)
- Hierarchical relations
- More-dimensional relations.

Hierarchical relations (Fig. 3.5) are built from dependent relations which contain not only their own surrogate but also the reference surrogate. The reference surrogate often represents the *Is_part_of* relationship and will be used for constructing the hierarchical structure.

In ORACLE there is a ROWID system attribute which has a unique value for each row. One problem is that it has a constant value only within one query and not during the lifetime of the row. Another problem is that one row does not represent the complete object very often.

Surrogate	Key	Attr 1	Attr 2

Figure 3.4 Concept of surrogate

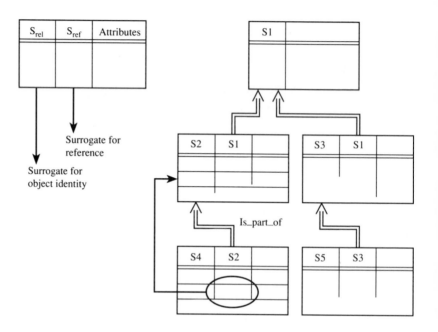

Figure 3.5 A dependent relation and a hierarchical relation

In dBASE the concept of indirect file name can be used. To build a hierarchical structure of relations (tables) we can store the names of child-tables into the fields of parent table. Then, we can use the mechanism USE(file_name) or USE&file_name. This concept can be used as a surrogate if we would represent every object by a special file containing only one record. This approach would not, of course, be very efficient. Concepts of object identity will be explained in more detail in Sec. 4.1.

3.3 COMPLEX OBJECTS

The concept of complex objects has been introduced in attempts to release the first normal form restriction of the relational model. A complex object can be thought of as an abstraction of a structure or a record in a programming language. It allows repeating groups, record nesting, and using a tree structure for storing its components. The simplest complex object can be an aggregate of components (also objects), each of which may have a different type. We will introduce this as a collection in later chapters about object-oriented programming.

The concept of complex object contains the following extensions:

- Sets of atomic values
- Sets of tuples (nested relations)
- Tuple-valued attributes
- General sets and tuple constructors
- Object identity
- Bitmap-valued attributes for storing multimedia data (storing pictures, fingerprints, X-ray photographs, audio signals, etc.).

In practice, we also use complex objects in simple applications.

Example
A foreigner entering another country is discussing his telephone number with the immigration officer when filling in a form.

```
Question: 'Do you have a telephone number?'
Answer:   'Well, I work for a building firm and every
          morning I am in my room on Number A. I am
          at a building site on Number B every
          afternoon. I have a telephone in my car—
          Number C. On working days I am in this
          town, where I have no telephone, but my
          neighbour John has Number D. At weekends, I
          live in the country where I can be reached
          on Number E.'
```

The immigration officer thought that he would be told only one number but he now has a complex data structure.

3.4 ITERATIVE AND RECURSIVE QUERYING IN NESTED RELATIONS

In Sec. 3.3 we described the research area concerned with removing the limitation of flat tuples by supporting structured objects instead. Another area of research deals with the limitation of traditional query languages. It has been proved that the relational query languages do not allow expression of the computation of the transitive closure of a relation. The reason is that the query has to be repeatedly applied and the number of steps is not known beforehand. In the relational model with underlying relational algebra, i.e. in SQL, tools are not available for writing a loop (except for a quantifier).

Consider an airport information system containing data about direct connections between airports. Using an SQL-like language we can define these connections as follows. We define the direct connections:

```
CREATE TABLE Connection (Start        CHAR(40),
                    (TABLE Destination   CHAR(40)));
Connection
Start       Destination
London      Paris, Frankfurt
Paris       Frankfurt, London
Frankfurt   London, Paris, Vienna
Vienna      Frankfurt, Rome
Rome        Vienna
```

```
Query:  Which cities can be reached directly from
        London?
    SELECT   Dest
    FROM     St IN Connection, Dest IN St.Destination
    WHERE    St.Start = "London";
```

We used two pointers. The first pointer St points to an element of the column Start and the second pointer Dest points to an element of the list Destination. If we ask an inverse query, i.e. we search all cities from which Frankfurt can be reached, we can write:

```
    SELECT   St
    FROM     St IN Start
    WHERE    EXISTS    "Frankfurt" IN St.Destination;
```

We can find all cities which are indirectly reachable with (at most) one change by using the following approach:

```
    SELECT X.Start, (SELECT YY.Dest
        FROM       Connection Y, Y.Destination YY
        WHERE      Y.Start IN (SELECT Destination
                                FROM X.Destination)
    FROM Connection X;
```

Obviously, the problem of computing all change connections cannot be solved by using the SQL because there may be arbitrarily long chains whose lengths have to be known in the compile-time.

Some theoretical approaches have been published, but the embedded mode of query languages will be used in applications. We will show this in Sec. 3.7.2 in an example of embedded SQL.

3.5 INTEGRITY CONSTRAINTS

One of the objectives of database technology is to provide means of maintaining control over and preserving the integrity of the database. As mentioned in Sec. 1.2, database integrity expresses a true mapping between the data and the real-world objects and their properties. The properties and relationships represented by data must be the same as in reality. In database programming the term 'integrity' has evolved to refer to the qualities of validity and consistency. Integrity is also concerned with illegal data accessing and modification.

The intent is to set up a number of integrity constraints on the data via special facilities available to them, and then for every update to make sure that the integrity constraints are satisfied.

Integrity is like security as far as the extent to which it is achieved and the cost of achieving it. The higher the degree of integrity, generally the higher the cost of achieving it in terms of the necessary software, access time, and storage cost. Thus, the intent is to achieve a satisfactory degree of integrity at a satisfactory cost. In fact, it may be practically impossible to avoid some invalid data values.

Example
If a new employee is hired and the secretary makes a spelling error when writing his or her name, there is no reasonable method of checking it.

There is no industry-wide standard for integrity, although a number of proposals have been suggested. In most applications, designers have implemented at least some degree of data validation at input time for some critical fields, e.g. checking that an entered value is in a given range of values (Month must be in the range 1...12). This level of protection is obviously important, and difficult to achieve reliably. It has been suggested that the specification of integrity rules could account for as much as 80 per cent of a database description. In some cases the validation mechanisms that have had to be developed are exceedingly specialized and sophisticated. The intent of database technology is to provide a wide range of easy-to-use generalized integrity mechanisms and avoid much of the traditional effort of implementing the mechanisms themselves, using them and enforcing them.

Integrity mechanisms must be provided with a set of integrity rules that define:

- What errors to check
- What to do if an error is detected

Integrity rules can be divided into two categories:

- Data validity
- Consistency

We will now outline some of the most important data validity and consistency constraints.

Data validity constraints are also called domain integrity rules. They concern acceptability of a value considered independent of its relationships to other values in the database.

- *Data types and format* A data field may be allowed to contain only values whose type and format must exactly match the characteristics declared for the data field in the schema.

Example
In dBASE we can write for purposes of the input data format checking the following clause in a @ . . . get statement:

```
@ 10,20   SAY       "Enter date MM/DD/YY:";
          GET       Year                 ;
          PICTURE   "99/99/99"
```

- *Value ranges* The value of a particular field may be required to fall within a certain range. For example, the month field must have values between 1 and 12. A field may be required to take only specified values. For example, dept_no can take only one of the five given values. It is usually implemented as a main part of the input data validation step prior to processing.

Example
In dBASE we can write, for purposes of the input data value checking, the following clause in a @ . . . get statement:

```
@ 10,20   SAY     "Enter MONTH:" ;
          GET      Month;
          RANGE    1,12
```

For checking the value entered in Month the clause range is used.

```
@ 10,22   SAY     "Enter DAY:" ;
          GET     Day;
          VALID   Day_in_Month;
          ERROR   "Wrong day number"
```

It is more difficult to check the number of a day in a month. Here, a user-defined Boolean function Day_in_Month has been used. If it returns false, the user-defined message in clause error will appear.

* *Uniqueness of a key field* Practically all DBMSs provide means of ensuring the uniqueness of a key of an inserted record.

Consistency constraints also concern the case in which two or more values in different tables in the database are required to be in agreement with each other in some way. The values of a data field in a given record may be required to appear also as values in some field of another record (or even perhaps in the same record). This type of constraint is also called referential constraint.

Example
Part_No in sold table must correspond to some Part_No in stock table, i.e. we cannot sell a part with non-existing Part_No.

This accomplishes two important tasks. First, whenever the Part_No field value is changed or added to the database by a command referring to either the Stock or Sold records, the DBMS must automatically introduce the same effect at both places. If this integrity constraint were not specified it would introduce serious integrity problems. Second, in some databases there is a virtual mechanism which provides apparent storage redundancy to application programs while actually avoiding internally the apparent storage redundancy. Internally the field is stored only once physically; all other appearances of the field are virtual and are materialized via some pointer mechanism.

* *Calculated fields* The value of a data field in a record may be required to be the result of a procedure using actual values of other fields. It may be called a calculated field and is materialized only at execution time and the value is not actually stored in the database.

Maintenance of data validity and consistency constraints entails much data checking. All update, insert and delete operations on the portion of the database with the constraints will have to be monitored. It may be very expensive for extensive constraints. Thus, the appropriate checking may be done more cost-effectively by means of a special utility program run periodically to perform the checking, rather than whenever the update operations occur. An important concern of the database administrator is setting up all these checking and monitoring methods.

3.6 TRIGGERS

Occasionally, it is necessary to incorporate side-effect-type mechanisms into the system. For example, it may be required that access to one table leads to changes in another; alternatively, it may be that the addition of a row to a table set results in the production of a report. A DBMS can support those facilities which are associated with a table and defines that when a particular condition involving information from that table occurs, then an action is induced. When such an event is triggered then a procedure is called to carry out the necessary processing. Parameters passed to the procedure can include a copy of the information which caused the event to trigger. In order to reduce the complexity of the system the DBMS allows any number of triggers to be associated with an entity set, but imposes a restriction that only one event can be associated with each trigger. The condition for checking is called a trigger condition, and the procedure representing the expected action is called a trigger procedure. Syntactically, we can write:

```
AFTER/BEFORE  <event>  CALL  <procedure>
```

Events can be specified as `store`, `delete`, `modify`, `get`.

Triggered procedures have applications in the area of maintaining integrity (consistency, constraints) and also in computing values of calculated fields, in enforcing authorization constraints, in selection of fields for insertion, in providing data encryption, in monitoring and tracing, in debugging, in compressing and decompressing data, in exception reporting. In dBASE-like systems there are not really any triggers but we can use the mechanism of the statement ON.

3.7 SIMPLE EXTENSIONS IN COMMERCIAL DBMSs

As shown, the use of the pure relational model is associated with serious shortcomings. The commercial DBMSs are not designed and implemented in the purely relational way. We will show the extensions on examples from the dBASE family (representing simple database systems) and from the SQL family (representing complex database systems). All these systems assume data in the first normal form.

3.7.1 Extensions in dBASE

The dBASE system was developed as a generalization of a file processing system and some of its former features are still included in it. It is important to say that these features are often very useful. We will discuss:

- Variables
- Heterogeneous arrays

- User-defined functions

Variables and arrays are used to store data found in files (in dBASE a table is implemented as a file). Variables are destined for storing single values. One-dimensional heterogeneous arrays can have the same structure as a record of a data file. This implies that two-dimensional arrays can be used for storing sets of the records found.

User-defined functions (UDF) are very powerful instruments which, however, can also be dangerous. A user-defined function can be called in an expression in a dBASE statement. This means that such a function call interrupts the execution of the dBASE statement and can cause some changes in the data structures used by the interrupted dBASE statement (e.g. the UDF can change the current record pointer). This can result in an inconsistency.

3.7.2 Embedded SQL and extensions in ORACLE

When using SQL we must remember that the relational model is set-oriented whereas the reality is object-oriented. When we describe each object as a record we can say that the data processing is record-oriented. All records in a file can be identical as far as their contents are concerned but they are still distinct objects having different physical addresses. Set-orientation does not take into account the order of elements in a set. These concepts are important to remember when using the clauses distinct and order by.

In data processing the order of records in a file is very important from an efficiency point of view. The use of indexing and clustering techniques is purely record-oriented and has nothing to do with relational algebra.

In those data processing features which are not supported in the relational model we need to perform operations on sets prepared by SQL. The concept of embedded SQL opens up the operational capabilities of the DBMS, i.e. in a C program we can ask SQL only to select specified rows from specified tables.

The fundamental idea underlying embedded SQL is that SQL statements (with various differences) can be used embedded in a program in some host language (C, Pascal, COBOL, FORTRAN, etc.). They can cooperate with host language variables (these variables have a preposition ':' in the SQL environment). The hybrid program consisting of host language statements and SQL statements will be translated by a preprocessor. SQL statements are usually introduced by EXEC SQL, i.e.:

```
EXEC SQL <SQL statement> ;
```

The preprocessor replaces SQL statements with specific procedure calls matching the host language syntax. After that, the generated program (completely in C, Pascal, etc.) will be compiled. In the following examples we will use a Pascal-like language without EXEC SQL (there is no standard).

In the simplest case, the result of a query will be a single number. We can store the number found using the into clause in the select statement.

Example

Query: How many first names do the department teachers have?

```
program Names;
    var
            Counter : integer;
begin
    SELECT    COUNT(DISTINCT NAME)
    INTO      :Counter
    FROM      DEPARTMENT;
    if SQLCODE = 0 then { OK }
            write ('Different first names :',
            Counter)
    else
            write ('Error');
end.
```

If we can be sure that only one row of the table (record) will be found, we can use the following construction.

Example

Query: Who is heading the given department?

```
program Head;
    var
            Dept _number : integer;
            TeacherName  : string;
begin
        read(Dept_number);
    SELECT    NAME
    INTO      :TeacherName
    FROM      EMPLOYEE
    WHERE     TEACHER_CODE IN
                    (SELECT    TEACHER_CODE
                     FROM      DEPT
                     WHERE     DEPT_NR = :Dept_number);
    if SQLCODE = 0 then
```

```
            write('The name is : ', TeacherName)
                 else
            write('Error');
  end.
```

In the following example, we will show the case of a `select` statement that selects a whole set of rows (records). These records can be made accessible successively by using a mechanism called cursor. The explanation of statements `declare`, `open`, `fetch`, `close` is given in program comments.

Example
Query: What are the names and the numbers of all departments?

```
program List;
      var
         DeptNumber : integer;
         DeptName : string;
begin
{ declares a cursor DEPT_CURS for a given table
and projection }
DECLARE DEPT_CURS CURSOR FOR
           SELECT   DEPT_NO, DEPT_NAME
           FROM     DEPT;
{ prepares the cursor DEPT_CURS for using }
   OPEN DEPT_CURS;
{ makes accessible the first tuple produced by the
previous SELECT }
   FETCH DEPT_CURS INTO :DeptNumber, :DeptName;
 { repeat fetching records until
   the last record not reached }
       while SQLCODE = 0 do
             begin
                print(DeptNumber,' ', DeptName);
                FETCH DEPT_CURS INTO :DeptNumber,
                :DeptName;
             end;
 { cancel using the cursor DEPT_CURS }
CLOSE DEPT_CURS;
end.
```

The next SQL extension, which we explain here, is so-called dynamic SQL. The principal idea is that we can construct the text of the SQL statement dynamically, i.e. at run time. This text has to be assigned to a string-variable defined in the host language environment which is often named SQLSOURCE. In the SQL environment a variable (often called SQLOBJ) will be declared into which the SQL statement will be translated. For this purpose the statement prepare exists in the SQL environment. Execution will be triggered by the SQL statement execute.

Example

The following program will ask for a statement and then perform it as if we input the statement from the keyboard in the interactive mode.

```
program Inter;
     var
           SqlSource : string;
begin
      DECLARE SQLOBJ STATEMENT;
      write('Query: ');
      read(SqlSource);
      PREPARE SQLOBJ FROM :SqlSource;
      EXECUTE SQLOBJ;
end.
```

FOUR

OBJECT-ORIENTED DATABASE SYSTEMS

In previous chapters we described shortcomings and desirable extensions of the relational DBMS. One approach to reaching the goals described consists in the use of object-oriented concepts in database technology. These concepts will be discussed in the rest of this book.

The main ideas of object-oriented programming will be discussed in detail in Part II. In this chapter we only briefly mention how object-oriented database systems offer solutions to the shortcomings described in Chapter 2. The object-oriented paradigm in database technology is based on the following fundamental concepts:

- *Object identity* Each real-world entity is modelled by a type of object. Each object is associated with a unique identifier and will be stored as a tuple of its subpart's object identifiers.
- *Complex objects* Each object has a set of instance attributes (instance variables) and methods; the value of an attribute can be an object or a set of objects. This permits arbitrarily complex objects to be defined as an aggregation of other objects. The set of attributes of an object and the set of methods represent the object structure and the behaviour, respectively.
- *Encapsulation* The attribute values represent the internal object's state. This state is accessed or modified by sending messages to the object to invoke its own corresponding methods.
- *Classes* Objects sharing the same structure and behaviour are grouped into classes. A class represents a template for a set of similar objects. Each object is an instance of some class. The concept of classes can be denoted as an extension of the concept of types (see Chapter 5).
- *Inheritance* A class can be defined as a specialization of one or more classes. A class defined as a specialization is called a subclass and inherits attributes and methods from its superclasses (see Chapter 5).

- *Overloading*   It is not necessary for different methods to have different names. One name can be used for different methods in different contexts if it is reasonable from the point of view of their semantics (see Chapter 5).
- *Late binding*   The decision as to which method should be used for the given object in the given context will be made dynamically (dynamic binding) at run-time (see Chapter 5).

An OODBMS can be defined as a DBMS that directly supports a model based on the object-oriented paradigm. It must provide persistent storage for objects and their descriptors (schema). The system must also provide a language for schema definition and for manipulation of objects and their schema. Other mechanisms known from the database technology (query language, indexing, clustering, concurrency control, multi-user access, recovery, etc.) must also be supported. Often, it will be required from an OODBMS to provide so-called version and schema evolution management. This property makes it possible for different versions of an object to be stored simultaneously and for the schema to be easily changed.

We will discuss these properties later (see Chapter 12).

4.1 OBJECT IDENTITY

In an OODBMS each object is uniquely identified by a unique object identifier (OID). The identity of an object has an existence independent of its value. Using OIDs allows objects to share subobjects and enables the construction of general object networks.

The concept of an object identifier is different from the concept of key in the relational data model. A key is defined by the value of one or more attributes and, therefore, can undergo modifications. In OODBMSs two objects are different if they have different object identifiers, even if all their attributes have the same values. Sharing objects in models where identity is based on value allows the applications to manage key values and the associated normalization problems. The concept of object identity introduces two different notions of equality among objects. The first is the identity equality (the same OID). The other is the value equality. Two objects can have different OIDs but all their value-attributes can have the same value and their object-attributes can be recursively value-equal.

There are three approaches to the construction of a OID:

- *Independent*   The OID is generated independently on the environment (GemStone).
- *Logical*   The OID contains the class name and the instance number

(ORION). This approach has the disadvantage that the object cannot change its class.

- *Physical*   The OID is derived from the disk address of the object (O_2). The class name is stored in the object itself. This approach has the following disadvantage. To determine whether a message sent to an object is valid for its class it is not enough to check the OID of the receiver but the receiver must really be fetched from disk. This means that non-valid messages cause useless disk access.

4.2 COMPLEX OBJECTS AND AGGREGATION

The values of an object's attributes can be other objects, both primitive and non-primitive. In principle, there are two possibilities for storing a complex object:

- *Direct*   The complex value is stored in the complex object. When complex values are supported by the model the system usually stores in the object attribute the entire complex value.
- *Indirect*   The complex value of an attribute is represented by an object and its OID is stored in the complex object. When the value of an attribute of an object O is a non-primitive object O', the system stores the OID of O' in O.

Using complex values as components is more efficient than using objects' OIDs. In this case, once object O is fetched, all components that are complex values are usually fetched as well.

In some applications we need to distinguish an aggregated subobject from a referenced subobject. The difference is, for example, in deleting. Subobjects given directly by aggregation will be deleted with the object, but with subobjects given indirectly by reference, only the pointers to them will be deleted.

When objects are used as components, the object O (a root of a complex object) contains only the OIDs of its components. Additional access messages may be needed to retrieve the component objects. In the case of multimedia data types, when the complex value is large (more than the page size) the value is not stored with the object of which it is a component.

Different constructors can be used in defining complex objects and values. A minimal set of constructors that should be provided by a model includes:

- Set
- List
- Tuple

A complex object can reference any number of other objects recursively.

An important relationship used in the concept of complex object is the *Is_part_of* relationship (aggregation), that is, the concept that an object is part of another object.

If the root of a complex object is removed, all component objects are deleted. In some systems a lock on the root of a complex object is propagated to all the components (see Chapter 12).

4.3 METHODS AND ENCAPSULATION

In general, a method description consists of two components. The first is the method specification, describing the method name, the names and classes of the arguments, and the class of the result, if any. This is not needed if type checking is executed at run-time. The other component is the method implementation, which consists of code written in a programming language. There can be other components present in the method definition (for example, trigger definitions).

Some systems provide access to the database from conventional languages (C, Pascal). In Chapter 7 the GemStone C Interface will be used to discuss this. Some OODBMS provide direct access to attributes by means of system-defined methods which have an efficient implementation. The drawback of the direct access is in danger of destroying consistency. The object's attributes should be manipulated through the object's methods only because there is nothing to protect the consistency when attributes of objects are accessible using a system-defined method. In OODBMSs characterized by distributed or client-server architectures an important architectural issue concerns the site where an invoked method is executed. Objects can be moved to the user's workstation and methods are then executed locally.

In all object-oriented database models each attribute is associated with a domain specifying the set of the possible objects that can be assigned to it as values (in so-called weak typed systems – see Chapter 5 – like GemStone this could be the most common class object with the semantical meaning any object). This set of objects has common semantics (e.g. a price) but its objects can be of different types (e.g. a price can be given as a fixed price by an integer number and also by a table specifying the dependence on bought parts). This suits certain programming languages, such as Smalltalk, in which instance variables do not have an associated type. For data management applications requiring efficient management of persistent data to allocate the appropriate storage and access structures the system should know the types of the possible values taken by the attributes.

An important question concerning instances and classes is whether the class membership of an object can be changed. The ability to change the class of objects provides support for object evolution. It lets an object change its structure and behaviour and still retain its identity. A domain-constraint problem arises when objects are allowed to change class. It can happen that an object O occurs as a value of an attribute A which should be from a given domain D. Then, after its change, the object O will not be type compatible with the domain D of attribute A. It is possible to place a tombstone in such an object indicating that this object changed its class but then the application must contain code to handle the exception.

Queries are issued on object collections. In some systems (ORION) the class not only acts as a template but also denotes the collection of all its instances. In other systems, constructors serve this purpose (GemStone).

4.4 PERSISTENCE

Persistence is a required functionality, which is obviously an important part of any DBMS. In OODBMSs, the persistence should be:

- Orthogonal to types, i.e. any data of any type can be made persistent at any time.
- Transparent, i.e. persistent and non-persistent data can be manipulated in the same way.
- Independent, i.e. the object manager of the OODBMS should automatically provide operations of explicit reading and writing of the objects from and to disk which are necessary for maintenance of data integrity.

The problem is that the structure of objects can differ greatly in each instance of one class and it does not fit the disk data structure (files, pages or physical blocks, records, etc). A mechanism should be available to define which object is persistent and which is non-persistent. This could be defined by explicit commands, by declaration in the database schema, or by reachability from a persistent object.

4.5 QUERY LANGUAGES

The object-oriented database systems use different object-oriented languages as query languages. For example, Objective-C (Iris), C++ (ONTOS, ObjectStore), COMMON LISP (ORION), Smalltalk resp. OPAL (GemStone). We will discuss the possibilities for these languages in Part II.

TWO

OBJECT-ORIENTED PARADIGMS

FIVE

CONCEPTS OF OBJECT-ORIENTED PROGRAMMING

5.1 INTRODUCTION

In this and the following two chapters we will explain the concepts of object-oriented programming and how these are used in programming languages (Pascal, C++, LISP and Smalltalk) and database technology (AutoLISP, OPAL). The Pascal-like languages (Pascal, C) are not very suitable or typical for object-oriented programming, but they are very popular (especially C++). Some object-oriented database systems are written in these languages and they are also used as query languages. We use them here for explaining the basic concepts of object-oriented programming. We start with an object-oriented version of Pascal because we assume that this will be the most acceptable language environment for most readers. In examples, we will use Turbo Pascal 6.0 and C++.

Traditional software development methods take the point of view that there are procedures and there are data structures which are treated as independent entities. An object-oriented system uses a class as an entity that represents both.

Object-oriented programming is a new style of programming in which data concerning an entity and associated procedures (actions on these data) is encapsulated to form an object. An object is a computing entity existing at a higher level than procedures or data structures.

To understand better the nature of an object it is helpful to consider first the nature of abstraction. To do so, think of the purpose of some real-world structures such as a TV or a computer. These are structured so that the commonly used things will be conveniently available by using a predefined interface, whereas those not frequently used are hidden. The idea of abstraction is extremely important. It supports concentrating on significant aspects and ignoring the rest.

5.2 OBJECTS AND ENCAPSULATION

The key concept of object-oriented programming is that a collection of data and the operations that are normally performed on that data are very closely related and should be treated as a single entity rather than as separate things. Most objects contain data and procedures. However, objects that consist of data only or procedures only are also possible. One can construct nested and hierarchical structures from objects.

Encapsulation adds procedures and functions to data structures of the object description. This means that we have not only data structures of the object but also methods which can be used for manipulation of this object. Usually, methods are the only way of accessing data.

Example
First, we show the traditional specifications for a sphere:

```
type Sphere =   record
                      R, X, Y, Z : real;
                  end;
procedure DefineLocation(var S : Sphere ;
                             X, Y, Z : real);
begin
        with S do begin X := X; Y := Y; Z := Z;
end;
end;
procedure DefineSize(var S : Sphere; R : real);
    begin
        with S do R := R;
    end;
procedure HowToRoll( . . . .); begin . . . end;
```

This can be encapsulated (Fig. 5.1 – Turbo Pascal 6.0) into:

```
type Sphere = object
        R : real;
        X : real;
        Y : real;
        Z : real;
```

```
procedure DefineLocation(X,Y,Z : real);
procedure DefineSize(R : real);
procedure HowToRoll( . . . .);
             end;
```

Implementation:

```
procedure Sphere DefineLocation(X, Y, Z : real);
begin
        X := X; Y := Y; Z := Z;
end;
```

Using:

```
var S1 : Sphere;
begin
    S1.DefineLocation(0,0,0); {using a method of
                              Sphere}
    S1.DefineSize(5);
    .
    .
    .
```

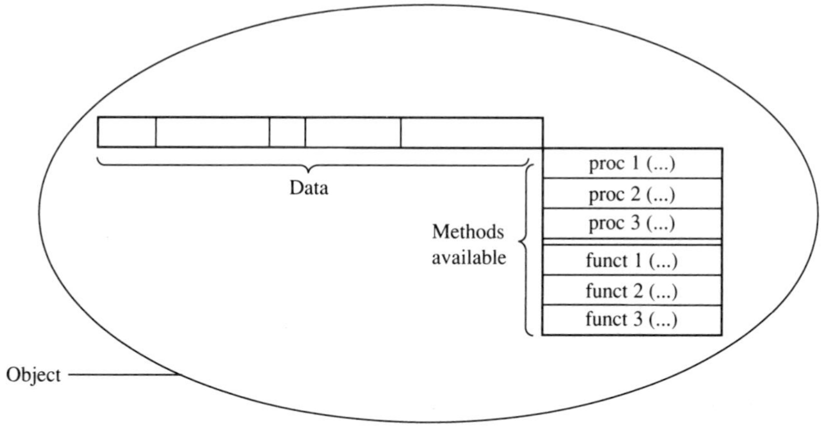

Figure 5.1 Encapsulation

5.3 CLASSES

Many different objects are identical with respect to their structure and capabilities. A common description of such objects is called a type in traditional programming languages (Pascal, C) or a class in object-oriented ones (SIMULA67, Smalltalk).

Object-oriented systems make a distinction between the description of an object (i.e. a class) and the object itself (i.e. an instance). A class represents a description of all its instances, i.e. a template for creating instances of this object type.

Every object is an instance of a class. The class therefore describes all the similarities of its instances. Each instance contains the information that distinguishes it from the other instances in instance variables. In uniformly object-oriented languages (e.g. Smalltalk) even a class is an object.

In this case the root of the entire class hierarchy is called object class (not in C++). This is the class from which all other classes are derived. The object class provides the capabilities expected of any object in the system, regardless of its specific purpose. If we do not put these common capabilities in the object class, then we will have to duplicate them in every single class we implement in order to achieve the same effect. In duplicating these functions across all our classes we are running a risk of making a mistake somewhere, and of leaving ourselves with many functions to debug when we make that mistake. This is what object-oriented programming is meant to prevent, as functions are packed into objects, and then are shared with all the other objects that need them, either through inheritance or by directly sharing instances of objects.

5.4 MESSAGES

Actions can be performed on objects by invoking one or more of the underlying methods defined in respective classes. Methods are the algorithms that represent the internal implementation of the behaviour of an object. These describe a single type of manipulation of an object's information (the response to a single type of message). A method, like a procedure, is the description of a sequence of actions to be performed by a processor.

The process of invoking a method in the class is called sending a message to the object. Methods are performed by an object after receiving a message. Messages perform a task similar to that of function or procedure calls in other languages.

However, unlike a procedure, a method cannot directly call another method. Instead, it must send a message. The important point is that

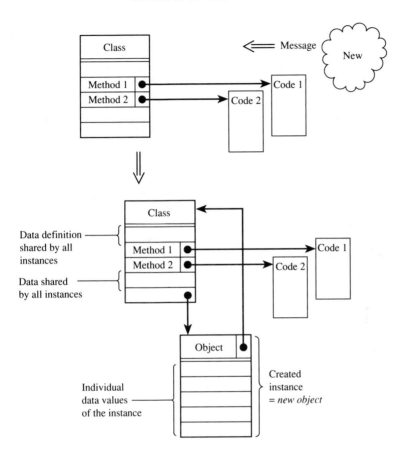

Figure 5.2 Creating a new object

methods cannot be separated from objects. When a message is sent, the receiver determines the method to execute.

5.5 INHERITANCE, OVERRIDING AND OVERLOADING

When a class (as an object) receives the message CreateNewObject (the name of such a message is language dependent), a new object with the capabilities described in the class is created (Fig. 5.2).

Classes are organized into a tree structure (single inheritance) or into a graph structure (multiple inheritance). In such a relationship, the predecessor is called the superclass and the successor is the subclass. A subclass inherits everything from its superclass. When an object is created as an instance of a class by sending a message CreateNewObject to this class, the created object only has not data structures and methods of the class it belongs to but it also inherits each of its data structures and methods from the superclass (and all predecessors of the superclass).

If superclass A has a method m(a:A) and a subclass C (derived from A) also declares a method having the same name and the same parameter list m(a:A), then the class C has overwritten the method m and we speak of overriding (we have only the current method). The overriding represents a redefinition of an inherited method.

If a subclass B (also derived from A) declares a method having the same name but a different list of parameters, e.g. m(s:String), then m is overloaded and we speak of overloading (we have one name for more things simultaneously, here we have one name for two visible methods).

The described mechanism used for implicit sharing on the class level in object-oriented systems is called inheritance. If a derived class inherits from only one superclass, then we speak of a single inheritance. In other cases there is multiple inheritance (see Sec. 5.12.2).

Methods can be overriden and overloaded. Overriding or overloading data structures is not permitted in most object-oriented systems. A new class can be derived by modifying an existing class and the following modifications can be made:

- Adding instance variables
- Providing new methods for some of the messages understood by the superclass
- providing methods for a new message (message not understood by the superclass).
- adding class variables.

Example
In this example we describe a simple hierarchical structure given in Fig. 5.3.

```
type 3d_point =  object
                      X, Y, Z : real;
                 end;
     Sphere     =  object(3D_point)
                       R : real;
                 end;
     MetallicSphere = object(Sphere)
                          ProducedOf: CodeOfMetal;
                      end;
```

Overriding methods builds a base for polymorphism.

Polymorphism is a concept which enables us to refer to objects of various classes at run-time using only one overriden procedure or function.

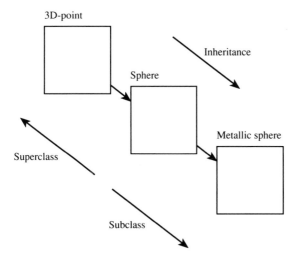

Figure 5.3 Hierarchial structure of classes and inheritance

This concept makes possible the description of the processing of objects whose type is not known at compile-time. As far as the object type compatibility is concerned, this means that instances of specialized types can be freely used instead of the more common types but not vice versa (e.g. in assignment, in mechanism of formal/actual parameters substitution). This means that a name of an action is shared up and down the class hierarchy but each class has or can have its own implementation of this action. We can use one overriden method (e.g. show) for objects of all types, and in each case the appropriate procedure will be used corresponding to the given type of object.

Example
The majority of cookery books are written in an object-oriented style.

```
type PanCake = object
                  Height : integer;
                  Radius : integer;
                  procedure HowToMix(<list of
                                ingredients>);
                  procedure HowToBake;
              end;
Pizza        = object(PanCake)}
                  procedure BasicLayer(<list of
                                ingredients>);
```

```
                virtual procedure HowToSeason;
                    end;
PizzaNapolitana
                = object(Pizza)
                        procedure LayerNapolitana(<list
                                        of ingredients>);
                        procedure HowToBake;
                virtual procedure HowToSeason;
                    end;
PizzaNapolitanaDeLuxe
                = object(PizzaNapolitana)
                        procedure DeLuxe(<list of
                                        ingredients>);
                virtual procedure HowToSeason;
                        procedure HowToServe;
                    end;
```

In this example, we can see that the class PizzaNapolitanaDeLuxe inherits the following procedures:

- HowToMix (transitive from PanCake)
- BasicLayer (transitive from Pizza)
- LayerNapolitana (direct from Pizza Napolitana)
- HowToBake (transitive from Pizza but overriden by PizzaNapolitana)

overrides the procedure HowToSeason, and adds the procedures DeLuxe and HowToServe. In Sec. 5.7 we explain the use of the keyword virtual in this example.

5.6 THE MECHANISM OF PROCESSING MESSAGES

Unlike data, an object can act. It can determine what to do when a message is received. When received by different objects the same message can cause completely different actions.

Objects, i.e. their data part, can be regarded as containers which can contain some values. They exist in time and can be created and destroyed.

Information is manipulated by sending a message to the object representing the information. When an object receives a message, it determines how to manipulate itself. The object to be manipulated is called the receiver of the message. A message includes a symbolic name that describes the type of manipulation desired. This name is called the message selector. The crucial feature of the message is that the selector is only a name for the desired manipulation. It describes what the programmer wants to happen, not how it should happen. The message receiver contains the description of how the actual manipulation should be performed.

We can use the following Smalltalk notation:

```
<receiver> <message selector:> [message arguments]
```

The programmer of an object-oriented system sends a message to an object to invoke a manipulation instead of calling a procedure.

In Pascal-like languages the process of sending a message will be described as a procedure call:

```
<receiver>.<message selector> (<arguments>)
```

where `<message selector>` corresponds to the name of a method defined in the class to which the object belongs.

A message names the manipulation. A procedure (a method) describes the details of the manipulation. Using a procedure name it will be specified exactly what should happen. A message, however, can be interpreted in different ways by different receivers. Therefore a message does not determine exactly what will happen; the receiver of the message does.

In addition to a selector, a message can contain other objects that take part in the manipulation. These are called message arguments. For example, to move a window, the programmer might send the object representing a window a message with the selector move. The message would also contain an argument representing the new location. Since this is an object-oriented system, the selector and argument are objects, the selector representing a symbolic name and the argument a location or point.

The set of messages an object can respond to is called its protocol. The external view of an object (it is nothing more than its protocol) represents its interface. The internal view of an object is like a data/procedure system. An object has a set of variables that refers to other objects (every single value is represented by an object).

In uniformly object-oriented languages (Smalltalk) the data structures of an object are update available only through methods, i.e. they are all private variables. There can also be private methods. Private methods defined in a class can be used only by methods defined in the same class and invoked inside one object.

The values of private variables play the role of data and the methods play the role of procedures. This distinction between data and procedures is strictly localized to the interior of the object.

If the representation used by a method is changed the method would also have to be changed, but only the methods in the object whose representation is changed need to be changed. All other methods will remain unchanged because they manipulate the object by sending it a message.

A subset of an object's private variables is called instance variables. The values of the instance variables are different from instance to instance and describe the internal state of the object.

The methods that describe the object's response to messages, i.e. its behaviour, are found in its class. All instances of a class use the same method to respond to a particular type of message. The difference in response by two different instances is a result of their different instance variables, i.e. it reflects their states.

The methods within a class use a set of names to refer to the set of instance variables. When a message is sent, those names in the method invoked refer to the instance variables of the message receiver. Some of an object's private variables are shared by all other instances of its class. These variables are called class variables and are part of the class.

In a system that is uniformly object-oriented a class is an object itself (not in C++, Turbo Pascal 6.0). A class provides the description of how objects (derived from this class) behave in response to messages. The processor running an object-oriented system inspects the receiver's class when a message is sent to determine the appropriate method to execute. For this use of classes it is not necessary that they be represented as objects since the processor does not interact with them through messages.

In a system under development a class provides an interface for the programmer to interact with the definition of objects. For this use of classes it is extremely useful for them to be objects so that they can be manipulated in the same way as all other descriptions. Classes are also the source of new objects in a running system. Here again, it is useful for the class to be an object, so that object creation can be accomplished with a simple message.

5.7 STATIC AND DYNAMIC BINDING

A simple implementation of run-time support system of an object-oriented language will be presented in Figs 5.4 and 5.5. We can see that procedures and functions defined as methods of a class have their code bound by a pointer to their names.

Each instance of a class has access to the code of the defined methods. The mechanism shown in Fig. 5.4 is called static binding. Each object contains a pointer to its class where pointers to the object-code of methods are stored.

Concepts of inheritance and overloading force one to make this mechanism more complex. We will show the reasons in the example from the previous cooking environment.

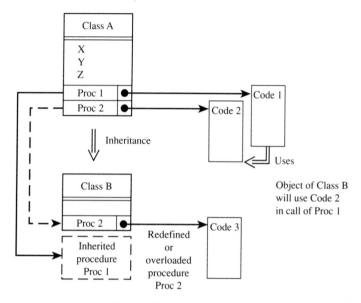

Figure 5.4 Static binding

Example
We use again the cooking environment example:

```
type PanCake = object
                Height : integer;
                Radius : integer;
                procedure HowToMix(<list of
                        ingredients>);
                procedure HowToBake;
            end;
   Pizza    = object(PanCake)}
                procedure BasicLayer(<list of
                        ingredients>);
        virtual procedure HowToSeason;
            end;
PizzaNapolitana
        = object(Pizza)
                procedure LayerNapolitana(<list
                        of ingredients>);
                procedure HowToBake;
        virtual procedure HowToSeason;
            end;
```

```
PizzaNapolitanaDeLuxe
    = object(PizzaNapolitana)
             procedure DeLuxe(<list of
             ingredients>);
      virtual procedure HowToSeason;
             procedure HowToServe;
      end;
```

As we can see, each `Pizza` has its own procedure `HowToSeason`. These procedures are only called in the procedure `BasicLayer` which is common for all pizzas. If the binding of the procedure `HowToSeason` were a static one the procedure `HowToSeason` from the class `Pizza` would be always used. This is not what we want. We need the specific procedures `HowToSeason` to be always used when the inherited procedure will be called. That is why the binding of the procedure `HowToSeason` must be a dynamic one.

Since the compiler cannot know in which context the procedure `BasicLayer` will be used it translates it with the call to `Pizza.HowToSeason`. The compiler does not know any other procedure `HowToSeason` at the time of compiling the procedure `Pizza.HowToSeason`. Therefore when the inherited procedure `BasicLayer`, defined in the environment of the class `Pizza`, uses the static bound procedure `HowToSeason` (which will be later overriden or overloaded), we will have a wrong seasoning when used for baking an object of the class `PizzaNapolitanaDeLuxe`. That is why we must have an extension of this mechanism – a dynamic binding (Fig. 5.5).

Procedures and functions which we assume could be used in this way we define as available for dynamic binding (in Turbo Pascal 6.0, we use the keyword `virtual`). In such a case their calling addresses will be substituted at run-time instead of at compile-time (as for static binding). We must tell the compiler that we intend to use many different forms of the same function, depending on exactly with what class of object we are dealing. In other words, the virtual functions at lower levels can inherit the capabilities of virtual functions at higher levels, leaving them free to do only what is necessary to change their behaviour.

In our example this means that all procedures `HowToSeason` will be defined as virtual. When the procedure `HowToBake` uses a call of a procedure `HowToSeason`, it has first to find which procedure `HowToSeason` is just actual, i.e. the recent one in the chain of overload procedures `HowToSeason`, and then to use its address.

The mechanism of the dynamic binding guarantees that the appropriate procedures from the bag of same-named procedures will be used, which matches the context of the object used.

Technically, a virtual function is only needed when a derived class

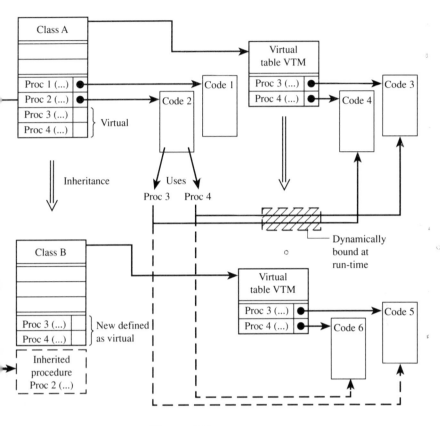

Figure 5.5 Dynamic binding

exactly duplicates the function name and the parameters of one of its base classes. The run-time penalty for declaring virtual functions is quite small, especially compared to the design and coding penalties that arise from not using them.

5.8 AUTOMATIC STORAGE MANAGEMENT

In general, almost all object-oriented programs generate objects which are used for a short period of time and then discarded. These short-lived objects usually represent the intermediate state of some computation, and when that computation is over, all pointers to the intermediate objects are lost.

As we have the possibility of creating and destroying objects we must realize that there has to be a mechanism which will take care to re-use memory. If new memory were allocated each time an object was constructed the system would very quickly exhaust all available memory. Objects which are occupying memory but which can no longer be used by any program are called garbage. There are two main classes of memory management algorithms: reference counting and garbage collecting methods.

The method known as reference counting uses the fact that a reference to an object is a pointer pointing to the object. Each object maintains a count of the number of currently existing references that point to the object. Care is taken to keep these counts accurate. When a reference count reaches zero there are no remaining pointers that can reach the object, and therefore the memory it occupies can be recycled for use by other objects. Free memory is maintained on free lists. A free list is a linear-linked list of free memory structures. When memory for a new object is required, the free list is first examined for object type. If an appropriate structure is found on the free list it is removed and used for the new object, otherwise a general memory-allocation routine is called to allocate new storage for the object. When the reference count on an object reaches zero the object is returned to an appropriate free list.

The main disadvantage of this method is that it cannot reclaim circular structures. If we consider a cyclic list (the last member of the list contains a pointer to the head of the list) then we see that if there is no pointer from the outside to this cyclic list, each element will be pointed by at least one pointer and the memory occupied by this structure cannot be re-used. Another problem is where to store the reference counts. Since we do not know beforehand how many references to an object will exist, we must estimate the upper limit. There is a significant overhead involved in using this method.

The method called garbage collection uses a different approach. We will briefly explain a garbage collection method known as stop and copy which is very popular, especially in LISP systems with virtual memory. The memory space used for a heap will be divided into two parts. The first part P1 (called *new space*) will be filled with newly created objects. If there is no free space left then the part P1 is renamed to *old space* and all accessible objects are copied into the second part P2 (called *copy space*) of the heap. After copying, all pointers to those objects must be updated. They have to point now to objects in *copy space P2* rather than to objects in *old space P1*. The first part P1 of the heap will be declared free and the whole process will start again, and only these parts will be mutually changed. New objects will now be created in P2, i.e. the *copy space* will now be called *new space*.

This simple method of garbage collection suffers from two main disadvantages:

- Memory will be wasted because one half of the heap memory will be used as the copy memory, i.e. not for new objects.

- Copying objects from the old space to the copy space causes a delay, i.e. the computation stops in order to perform a garbage collection. Such a pause can take several minutes. This is particularly unacceptable in systems that have response time requirements. It will not be recommended to use systems with garbage collection in real-time embedded systems.

Memory management is a central task in object-oriented systems. Because a large percentage of execution time is spent on performing this task, a great deal of attention has been devoted to speeding up the operation of the memory manager.

The object memory provides the object-oriented system with an interface to the objects that make up a virtual image. Each object is associated with a unique object identifier also called its *object pointer*. The communication about objects between the object manager and the object-oriented system is based on using object pointers. The object memory associates each object pointer with a set of other object pointers. Every object pointer is associated with the object pointer of a class. If an object has instance variables its object pointer is also associated with the object pointers of their values. The individual instance variables are referred to by integer indices. The value of an instance variable can be changed, but the class associated with an object (usually) cannot.

The object manager provides the following fundamental functions to the object-oriented system:

- Access the value of an object's instance variable. The object pointer of the instance and the index of the instance are arguments and the object pointer of the instance variable's value is returned.
- Modify the value of an object's instance variable. In this case the object pointer of the new variable must also be given.
- Access an object's class.
- Create a new object.
- Find an object's number of instance variables.

Objects no longer used are reclaimed automatically when there are no object pointers to them from other objects.

5.9 RE-USABILITY

Developments in software engineering have resulted in a system design methodology based on object-oriented concepts. The primary benefit of this methodology is that it raises the level of abstraction in the design process so that the objects are re-usable. This means that objects represent functional packages, requiring no additional work on the part of the programmer to use them. This idea is contained in libraries of functions and procedures in many languages but only if combined with dynamic binding do they allow us to extend predefined classes without studying their details. The primary idea is that the programmer will use catalogues of ready, predefined classes in the same way as hardware designers.

5.10 STRONG TYPING AND WEAK TYPING

C++ and Pascal are strongly typed languages, where the exact type of each object is explicitly stated in the source code of the program. Users must specify exactly the type of each variable they use and the compiler provides type checking at compile-time, i.e. it checks the types of the objects to ensure that all demanded operations can be executed. The compiler will also assume that there is no need to keep the type information around. This compiler is based on a strong typing model. In these languages, there is no built-in capability to provide run-time checking.

At first, such a capability would be suitable for processing heterogeneous collections. Such collections can hold arbitrary objects, regardless of their types. We must have some mechanism for checking the types of objects at run-time, because what we do with individual objects within the collection will most likely depend on what kinds of objects they are. This problem is solved by using the concept of polymorphism in object-oriented programming. Using overriden methods, we can manipulate an object without knowing its class in compile-time if it is an instance of classes related by specialization. We send a message corresponding to an overriden method which has different implementations for different types of objects. The object-receiver makes the choice of the suitable implementation itself.

Many object-oriented languages (Smalltalk, LISP) are built on the concept of weak typing. This means that the system does not check the types of data used in the program at the compile-time, instead it depends on the running system to detect problems that arise from type conflicts. In these systems one must have the capability of checking the type of an object at run-time. The relative advantages of strong and weak typing are still subject to much disagreement. Weak typing leads to very flexible systems that may easily be extended. However, it also results in programs whose total behaviour is difficult to validate because so much is dependent on the run-time system and so little help is received from the compiler. Weak typing requires much of the system to be supported by a run-time environment, which takes a percentage of the computer's time to support, i.e. the overhead is large.

Strong typing systems do not introduce this overhead to such a degree, as most of these issues are resolved at compile-time. These systems produce programs where the compiler has done a great deal of work to verify that all the individual operations are legal, and that all codes operate on clearly defined types of data. Strong typing also produces programs that are more difficult to modify because they are less flexible. On the other hand, the compiler relieves the user from manually validating the impact of his or her changes.

A good practice is to design and develop an application using a weak typing system. Once debugged, the application can be moved to an environment where strong typing is used by discarding some of the capabilities found in a uniformly object-oriented environment and replacing them with static logic.

5.11 OBJECT-ORIENTED CONCEPTS IN TURBO PASCAL

In this section we will briefly outline how the concepts of the object-oriented programming were implanted into Pascal. We use Turbo Pascal 6.0 (Borland) here, which is an object-oriented extension close to Object Pascal promoted by Apple Computers.

The general syntax for declaring a class is as follows:

```
type
    <class name> = object (<parent class name, if any>)
                <list of data fields declarations>
                <list of procedures and functions headings>
end;
```

Names of fields of subclasses must be unique. Procedures and functions represent the object's methods and are only specified as if they were declared forward. After classes are defined, their procedures and functions must be declared. The name of the class qualifies (delimited by the dot operator) the name of the defined (and also the name of the used) procedure or function.

```
procedure <class name>.<procedure name> (<list of
                parameters>);
                <tail of declaration of the procedure>
```

The class data fields may directly be accessed in this method. Turbo Pascal allows overriding and overloading methods of static objects.

For disconnected classes that are contained in a library unit one can use the same names for methods as well as for data fields. As long as one explicitly qualifies the data fields and methods with the names of the objects, no confusion can occur. Turbo Pascal does not support automatic initialization of objects (as does C++, see Sec. 5.12). Static objects are automatically created and removed, like static variables. They are compiled into machine code that runs faster than that of dynamic objects. On the other hand, dynamic objects offer more run-time flexibility and support polymorphism. The main mechanism for dynamic objects involves virtual procedures and functions (the keyword `virtual` will be used). Virtual methods are related to constructors, which are methods used for creating the link to the table called the Virtual Method Table during the initialization of the object.

Once a method has been declared as virtual in a class, it must be declared virtual in all subclasses. Virtual methods must have the same parameter list in every class in which they are used. A constructor must be called for initializing objects with virtual methods and it can be inherited. For deleting an object with virtual methods a destructor has to be called for proper cleanup of the heap. The destructor reads the run-time size of the object to be deleted and tells it the dispose procedure. It can be inherited.

When a class is implemented in a unit the declaration of the class is placed in the interface part, while the detailed coding is put in the implementation segment.

Assigning objects is allowed, but with the following limitation: an object of a subclass can be assigned to another object of an ancestor class, but not vice versa. The reason for this rule is that subclasses have more fields than their ancestor classes and we can perform the movement only when all fields of the destination have been assigned.

Objects can be parts of records. Such records are used when a group of objects is managed using a data structure, such as a linked list, stack, etc. Since these structures are most frequently implemented as dynamic data, dynamic objects will be used.

Dynamic objects use extended predefined `New` and `Dispose` procedures. The extension is made due to dynamic binding (virtual methods, constructors, and destructors).

```
new(<pointer>, <constructor>(<list of param.>));
dispose(<pointer>,<destructor>(<list of param.>));
```

5.12 OBJECT-ORIENTED CONCEPTS IN C++

The C++ language (as an extension of C) supports the ideas of object-oriented programming but is not a pure (or uniformly) object-oriented language, i.e. the mechanism object, message is not the only one used.

5.12.1 Classes

The definition of a class in C++ has the following form:

```
class <class name> {
        private:
                <type_1> <private_var_1>;
                . . .
                <type> <private_var>;
                <private_method_1>;
                . . .
                <private_method>;
        public:
                <type_2> <public_var_1>;
                . . .
                <type> <public_var>;
                <public_method_1>;
                . . .
                <public_method>;
        protected:
                <type_3> <protected_var_1>;
        . . .
        <type> <protected_var>;
        <protected_method_1>;
        . . .
        <protected_method>;
};
```

The keywords *private, public*, and *protected* control access to class members, i.e. to data structures (instance variables) and methods (procedures and functions), in the following way:

- *Private*   Class members can be used only by member methods of the same class, or by friends of that class (see later in this section).
- *Public*   Class members can be used by any method.
- *Protected*   Class members can be used by members and friends of derived classes.

Example
Definition of a class:

```
class collection {
private:
        char* description;
        int acquired_date;
```

```
public:
     void initial(char*, int, int, int);
     void in_Year(int);
     void subject(char*);
     void print();
};
```

Specification of a method:

```
void collection::print()
{
     cout << collection::description <<
     " acquired at: " \
          << collection::date
};
```

In each method of a class, a pointer this is defined. This points to the instance of this class which is current in this particular method.

The specification *private* is a default. Sometimes it is necessary for a method to be able to access private data from more classes. In C++ there is a construct called a friend which makes this possible. A function is made a friend of a class by a friend definition in that class.

Example

```
class collection {
private:
     char*    description;
     int      acquired_date;
public:
     friend void look(collection, invoice);
};
class invoice {
private:
     char*    invKey;
     char*    description;
     int      paid_date;
public:
     friend void look(collection, invoice);
};
void invoice::look(collection x, invoice y)
{
     . . . x.acquired_date . . . ;
     . . . y.paid_date ....... ;
};
```

If a derived class has access to the private data structures of its parent class these private data structures of the parent class must be defined as protected.

5.12.2 Multiple inheritance

The class hierarchy will be expressed in C++ in the following way:

```
class a { ................................
}
class b: public a {//class b is derived from class a
.............................................
}
```

In this case, all public data of class a will be public-accessible also in class b. If the keyword public is omitted, the public data of a will be private in b.

In C++ the concept of multiple inheritance can be used. This means that the derived class can inherit data and methods from more than one parent class.

```
class x: public x, public y { . . . };
```

Since all data and methods (also denoted as class members) in a derived class must be unambiguous, it is not possible to inherit methods with the same names from more parent classes. In such a case the qualification must be used, i.e. we have to use a fully qualified member name in the following form:

```
class_name A::A member_name
```

Object-oriented programming methodology includes a concept of using many small functions and procedures. This can lead to inefficiencies because the cost of calling a function can be comparable with the amount of memory references and assignments needed for the body of a trivial function. The inline function facility handles this problem. This means that the code of the inline function will be directly inserted instead of being called.

An object's elements and functions can be referred to in the same way as in Pascal:

```
code = instance.codeTeacher;
```

To distinguish between private and public parts of an object, the keyword public will be used in C++. The compiler assumes that until it sees this keyword no one except the methods of a class has access to any of the defined variables or functions.

```
class a {
                int codeTeacher;
                char *string;
           public:
                int searchFunction(int);
                void insertTeacher( . . . );
     }
```

What private parts of objects provide is a means of segregating the dangerous data within a class and restricting access to it.

The concept of constructors and destructors in C++ is similar to that in Pascal. They are called during execution of new and delete. In C++ no special keywords exist for these purposes, but the constructor is a method with the name of the class, and destructor has the class name with the prefix ~.

Example
```
class collection {
     . . .
     public:
          collection() { . . . }; // Constructor
          ~collection() { . . . }; // Destructor
          . . .
     };
```

5.12.3 Constructors and destructors for static objects

Traditionally, we have global static and local static variables in C and also global static and local static objects in C++. The keyword static is used for this purpose.

Example
```
     // global static object
          static collection sword( . . . );
     // local static object
          void xyz()
          {
                static collection subject( . . . );
          };
```

Free store objects can be handled by using the operators new and delete.

Example

```
class stack {
  int* top;
  int* bottom;
  int  size;
public:
  stack(int s) { top = bottom = new int[size = s]}
  ~stack() { delete[size] bottom; }
  void push(int i)
  {
        if (( top - bottom) < size)
            *top++ = i;
  }
  int pop()
  {
        if ( top > bottom)
            return *(-top);
  }
};
```

In some applications an instance of a class A is used in the private data part of the definition of class B (an object is a member of the data part of another class). The constructor of class B must know the values which are necessary for the instance of class A to be initialized. In the following example the object of the class point describes a centre of an object of the class circle.

Example

```
class point {
  int coord_x;
  int coord_y;
public:
      point(int x, int y) {coord_x = x; coord_y = y; }
  . . .
};

class circle {
  point centre;
  int radius;
public:
      circle(int centre_x, int centre_y, int radius)
    :
```

```
        centre(centre_x, centre_y) { . . . }
        . . .
};
```

5.12.4 Using C++ libraries

C++ and its standard libraries are designed for re-usability. In class libraries, classes form a graph (not only a single tree derived from a common root) which is given by multiple inheritance. The class library is a large collection of standard classes that implement standard programming units that can be used as building blocks to create new programs. C++ leaves it to the individual developers to do so. However, there are many libraries which can be used. The problem is that there is no standard. The advantage of this approach is that the overhead is not so large as in the case of uniformly object-oriented languages, i.e. we link only that code to our application which is necessary and which will be really used.

C libraries (and most tools that support programming in C) can be also used from a C++ program.

Re-using code is one of basic idea behind object-oriented programming. We try to re-use existing code wherever appropriate. Declaring predefined header files, one directs the linkage editor to include the appropriate module from C++ library files.

Class definitions from C++ libraries can be used in two major ways:

- Class composition
- Class derivation

Class composition is the simplest method of re-using class code. In plain C this is the only possibility. One can re-use library functions and procedures in their original form, i.e. one tries to compose one's application from library functions calls like a wall is constructed from bricks. Bricks are of fixed shape and size which cannot be changed. One uses statements of programming languages as the mortar.

Class derivation uses the inheritance concept. This allows addition of new, desired data structures and functionality to the class definitions from the library and the creation of new, derived classes. C++ supports a completely generalized type – an abstract class. The abstract class defines a concept but not a template for creating objects, i.e. it can be used only for deriving new classes. We can imagine that we can change the mould for producing bricks and produce bricks that would be especially suitable for our building. If we have to build a house it is not easy to say how to design the size and shape of the bricks in order to make the building process as easy as possible. In programming there is, in principle, the same difficulty.

The main problem of class libraries is their standardization, i.e. the fact that there is no standard at all in C++ libraries. Every C++ compiler producer prefers its own libraries and its own system of predefined classes. Portability is a problem.

5.13 SUMMARY

The main features of the object-oriented philosophy are information hiding and data abstraction represented by encapsulation, message passing, inheritance, polymorphism, dynamic binding, and automatic storage management. Object-oriented languages have many advantages compared with more traditional imperative, procedure-oriented languages. The primary advantage is that the inheritance mechanisms of object-oriented language enables codes to be re-used in a convenient manner, and this can improve programmer productivity. This has the advantage of reducing overall code bulk and increasing a programmer's productivity, since one has to write less original code. Inheritance enhances code factoring, which means that a code for performing a particular task is found in only one place, and this eases the task of software maintenance. Information hiding and data abstraction increase reliability and help to decouple procedural and representational specification from implementation.

Object-oriented languages have a few characteristics that are considered to be disadvantages. The primary disadvantage is the run-time cost of using them. Also, for a simple operation a message must be sent, received and processed in uniformly object-oriented languages. It would certainly take more machine instructions than the classical approach. This is why the message-passing mechanism is implemented for actions up to a certain level of abstraction.

The major disadvantage is the run-time cost of dynamic binding mechanism. Also, sending a message takes more time than a straight function call. Some studies have shown that with a well-implemented message manager this overhead is approximately 1.75 times a standard function call. Often, some of the work done automatically by a message-send must be carried by the programmer in any case, using code surrounding function calls or even multiple function calls.

Another disadvantage is that implementing an object-oriented language is more complex than implementation of a comparable procedure-oriented one, since the semantic gap between these languages and typical hardware architecture is wider. Therefore more software simulation is required.

A significant problem of using object-oriented languages is that the programmer must learn an often extensive class library (e.g. 300 classes) before becoming proficient. As a result, object-oriented languages are more dependent on good documentation and development tools.

SIX
CONCEPTS OF OOP IN LISP AND AutoLISP

6.1 STRUCTURES IN LISP

A very short introduction to LISP will be given in this section. (LISP programmers should skip it.)

The LISP programming language was conceived in 1960. It has been linked with the development of artificial intelligence for which it has been the major programming language. Since 1960, considerable improvements have transformed this language.

In the recent database technology, COMMON LISP (Steele, 1984) with COMMON LISP Object System (Keene, 1989) will be used also for implementing object-oriented databases (e.g. the often-cited ORION database system has been implemented in COMMON LISP on a Symbolics 3600 LISP machine), and AutoLISP (also based on COMMON LISP) will be used for storing and manipulating geometrical objects in CAD-databases on IBM PC-compatible machines. In this context it should be mentioned that a PC machine using 80386 can theoretically address 4 GB extended memory which can be enough for many CAD applications.

The name of the language is an abbreviation of LISt Processing. The core of the LISP-system comprises the *atom* (primitive object) and the *list* (compound object). An atom is represented by a chain of characters and it is a basic and indivisible piece of information. Groups of information are organized in the form of lists. A list can contain only atoms or lists as its elements.

The LISP language is based upon the convention that LISP programs are represented by lists composed of functions calls. An element of a list consists of a pair of function names and function arguments. Any of the arguments can be a function call.

```
(<function-name> <list-of-arguments>)
```

For manipulating lists, LISP has the following basic (and many other) operators (used as functions):

- Constructors which make compound objects.
- Selectors which decompose compound objects.
- Predicates which determine the type of value of objects in run-time. LISP is built on a concept of weak typing and the type is bound to the value, not to the variable.

The most primitive constructor in LISP is cons. This expects two arguments and returns a new list which is built by adding the first argument to the front of the list passed as the second argument. Before we give an example we must explain the evaluation. When accepting an atom during evaluation of arguments LISP assumes that it has received a name of a function. If this is not our intent we have to quote the argument with the character ' or with quote. Quote will be used to determine whether we wish to use a LISP expression as a piece of data or as a program. An expression referred to as a program will be evaluated as a *function call*.

Example
The LISP notation is illustrated in Fig. 6.1. In this example we can see how the constructor cons works. The following LISP program:

```
(cons '(A ((B C) D))) or
(cons (quote(A ((B C) D)))) =>
```

creates the compound object in Fig. 6.2.

As we have seen, the list created by cons has no name. For this purpose the construction setq will be used which performs an assignment:

```
(setq mylist (quote (A (B C) D)))
```

If we write

```
(setq prg (* 13 14))
```

we immediately obtain (LISP will be interpreted in most cases) a value of the product 182. Afterwards, if we write

```
prg
```

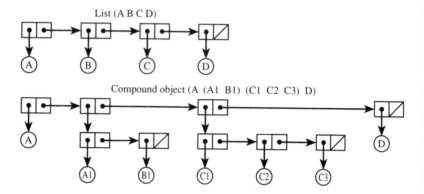

Figure 6.1 Lists and notation in LISP

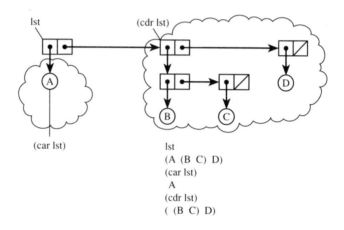

Figure 6.2 Functions Car and Cdr

we obtain 182 again.

The first element of the list can be examined with the function `car`. This is a function which expects a single list as an argument and returns the first element of that list. The original list is not altered in any way.

The function `cdr` also expects a single list as an argument, but it returns a list consisting of all but the first element of the given list, i.e. it returns the rest of the list. The original list will not change.

Example
```
mylist => (A (B C) D)
(car mylist) => A
(cdr mylist) => ((B C) D)
```

6.2 FUNCTIONS IN LISP

A LISP program is a list. Lists are evaluated according to the first element of the list to a function definition, to a function call, or to data. If the first element of the list is a function name, then other elements are arguments of this function. These arguments can be complex structures or function calls. Such a list will be called a *form* in LISP and its elements are called *terms*.

When a program is entered, the LISP interpreter evaluates its value. It evaluates an atom by looking for the object that it stores. It evaluates a form by first assessing all the terms in the form and then applying the function (its name is given by the value of the first term) to its arguments. *Integers*, *reals*, and *strings* will be evaluated on their own. *Symbols* will be evaluated to the value of their current binding, i.e. according to the object they currently represent. Exceptions exist, e.g. the function quote which does not evaluate its argument but returns it as it is.

It is often necessary to determine when two pieces of data are equal to each other. The concept of equality is not quite as simple as it first appears. We need to understand the difference between an *object* and an *object reference*, i.e. between equality comparison and identity comparison. Two objects cannot be equal because each exists independently of the other and each has its own identity. We can have either two different object references to the same object or two objects, where one is a copy of the other.

All types of data and programs in LISP are known as objects. When a function wishes to return an object it does not return an object but an object reference. It is a *pointer*, and it describes the place in memory which holds the object itself.

The function eq tests if two object references refer to the same object (identity comparison). It expects two arguments. If the two arguments both evaluate the same object then eq will return the symbol T, i.e. true. If we type in the same list twice, we obtain two unique objects, and thus they are not equal in the sense of the function eq.

If we want to know whether two objects are equal in the same sense that two copies of one template are equal (equality comparison), we have to use the function equal. For numeric arguments predicates >, <, >=, <=, and = can be used.

The special form defun allows us to define a new function.

```
(defun <name of function> (<list of parameters>)
                          (<body of function>)
)
```

The body of the function contains the formula for actually computing the value of the function from passed arguments.

When a function is called, LISP temporarily associates the names of parameters (i.e. formal parameters) with the values of the arguments (i.e. actual parameters) given in the call. We say it creates *bindings*, which last during the function call. When the call is complete, the bindings are undone, and names of the parameters will be given the former value (perhaps no value at all).

Function if represents the conditional statement. It expects three arguments. The first argument (test) is always evaluated. The result of evaluating the test is used to decide which of the other two arguments should be evaluated. It is similar to the *if . . . then . . . else* statement from the Pascal environment.

The main weapon of LISP is the *recursive function*. We assume that the reader is acquainted with the recursive function concept from Pascal-like languages. It should be emphasized that recursion means defining a concept in terms of itself.

Example

A very popular recursive function is append. This appends the second argument to the first (both are lists). This example is very often shown in examples in any language with recursivity. We will show it too, but it must have a different name because append is a predefined function in COMMON LISP.

```
(defun append-extra (head tail)
            (if (null head)
            tail
            (cons (car head)
                  (append-extra (cdr head)
                  tail)))))
```

Function null tests if its argument is an empty list. We can see that when a list should be appended to an empty list the result is known in the first step. It is the list given as the second argument. Otherwise, the first element from the first argument will be taken, and the function append-extra will be called again, this time with the shortened first argument.

Recursive programming is a topic dealt with in many good books and it is not the main concept of object-oriented programming used in object-oriented database systems. On the other hand, all languages used in object-oriented programming use this concept.

Except for functions, global variables can be defined using the function defvar:

```
(defvar *<name of variable>*
```

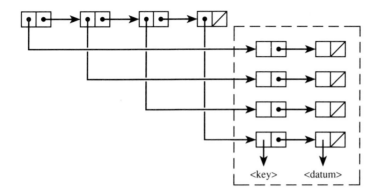

Figure 6.3 An association list

```
'(<initial value of variable>)
"<documentation string>"
)
```

If we need to give names to results which may be needed later or more than once, we use the function let:

```
(let ((<name-1> <expression-1>)
      (<name-2> <expression-2>)
        .
        .
        .
      (<name-n> <expression-n>))
     <body>
)
```

Each name given in let is bound to the result of evaluating the corresponding expression. After these bindings have been made, the body is evaluated.

6.3 ASSOCIATION LISTS

An association list (abbreviated to a-list) is a specially structured list whose elements are other lists (Fig. 6.3).

The car of each sublist is called a *key* while the cdr of each sublist is called a *datum*. The value of a key can be found using the function assoc. This function expects a key and an a-list as arguments and it returns the entire sublist associated with the key (or nil representing in this case an empty value in LISP). The datum can be obtained using the function second for extracting it.

Example

```
(setq schedule '((Brown Algebra Calculus)
                 (Crown Geometry)
                 )
      )
(assoc 'Brown schedule) => (Brown Algebra Calculus)
(cdr (assoc 'Brown schedule) = > (Algebra Calculus)
```

Association lists are frequently used for storing data that can be accessed by a key. This is similar to arrays in other programming languages. We can imagine how an array with the first column containing a key can be transformed into an a-list.

Considering the object-oriented principles of the real world we should be able to

- Make a new object using a constructor function
- Separate its parts using an accessing function
- Set or modify values stored in the object's fields
- Decide if two objects are equal using a predicate.

One simple way to accomplish this is to represent an object as a list of items containing all parts and names of the functions concerned. Defining these functions is quite tedious. There is the special form `defstruct` which allows us to define new structures easily:

```
(defstruct object var-1 var-2)
```

The first argument to `defstruct` is the name of the structure which we wish to define. The remaining arguments are the names of the fields which we want this structure to have. Fields in a structure are called *slots* in LISP. This function has many side-effects. Its call causes the following new functions to be defined:

- A constructor function `make-object`.
- The accessing function `object-var-1`, `object var-2`.
- The predicate `objectp` which returns T if its argument is an object of this kind.
- A function `copy-object` which returns a copy of the object which it is passed.

The function `setf` is actually a generalized updating function which can destructively modify a part of an object. The first argument of `setf` must be an accessing form while the second is the new value. When we apply the `setf` to a symbol we update its value. When we apply the `setf` to the accessed slot of an object we change its value.

There is a different concept of data typing in LISP to that in Pascal-like languages. Data is typed, not variables. Data type of any object can be determined at run time. The special form `defstruct` not only allows us to define new structures it also integrates these structures into the type system. Types (in the object-oriented terminology we would say *classes*) defined by `defstruct` are subtypes of the predefined type `structure`.

The concept of generic functions in LISP is similar to function overloading in languages such as C++.

Dispatching to a subfunction based on the type of one or more arguments is so common that LISP supplies the macro `typecase` to make such codes simpler. It branches according to the type of its key.

Example
```
(defun test-of-type (n)
          (typecase n
              (fixnum 'integer)
              (float  'real)
              (t      'sorry, neither integer nor
              real)))
```

6.4 OBJECT-ORIENTED PROGRAMMING IN CLOS

The object-oriented concepts from different LISP dialects have been collected and the CLOS (COMMON LISP Object System) has been built (Bobrow *et al.*, 1988). CLOS is an extension to COMMON LISP for object-oriented programming. It is intended to be included in the forthcoming ANSI Standard for COMMON LISP. A detailed description of CLOS is beyond the scope of this book. One is given in Keene (1989) and a complete example extending over 40 pages is given in Booch (1991). This section provides only a brief introduction to CLOS and will mainly describe how to:

- Define a class
- Define an instance variable
- Define a class variable
- Define a method
- Create an object
- Initialize an object
- Access the instance variables of an object
- Use directly defined and inherited methods.

6.4.1 Class definition

Classes are defined by using the `defclass` macro:

```
(defclass <class name> (<list of superclasses>)
         (<list of instance variables descriptions>)
)
```

We see that it is possible to define not only one superclass as in Turbo Pascal (single inheritance) but more than one superclass (multiple inheritance). Instances of the new class include all the instance variables defined in all the inherited classes, and all operations defined for the inherited classes can also be used on the new class.

In the LISP terminology an instance variable will be called a slot. In the simplest case we use only names of instance variables in their list in defclass macro.

Objects can be created by using the make-instance function:

```
(make-instance <class name>)
```

Class name can be used as a type name to check the type of an object (predicate typep).

Example
```
(defclass teacher () (code name age salary))
(setq john (make-instance 'teacher))
(typep john 'teacher) => t
```

For being able to assign a value or to display a value of an instance variable we need an access function to its address, i.e. a tool for referencing it. For this purpose, the slot-value function is available:

```
(slot-value <class-name> <name of instance variable>)
```

Using predicate slot-boundp we can test whether an instance variable has a value bound.

Example
```
(setq    mary (make-instance 'teacher))
(setf    (slot-value mary 'name) mary)
(setf    (slot-value mary 'salary) 2000)
(print   (slot-value mary 'salary)) => 2000
(slot-boundp mary 'age) => nil
```

We can use the with-slots macro for referencing more instance variables of one object. Its meaning is similar to the construction *with . . . do . . .* in Pascal.

Example
```
(with-slots (name salary) mary (setq name 'mary)
                                (setq salary 2000)
)
```

The `with-slots` macro can also be used for renaming instance variables of different objects of the same class.

Example
```
(with-slots ((salary-john salary) (age-john age))
john
(with-slots ((salary-mary salary) (age-mary age))
mary
    ( . . . what to do . . . )
))
```

In the simplest case we use only names of instance variables in their list in class definition. If we wish to describe some properties of instance variables we substitute each instance variable by a list consisting of its name and its properties (called slot options in CLOS), e.g. to be initialized by an explicit value given in `make-instance` when an object is created (*:initarg* slot option in CLOS), to be initialized by a default value when an object is created (*:initform* slot option in CLOS).

Example
```
(defclass soldier () ((sex :initarg :sexval :initform
"M")
                    . . .
            ))
(slot-value (make-instance 'soldier) 'sex) => "M"
(slot-value (make-instance 'soldier :sexval "W")
'sex) => "W"
```

Except for the `slot-value` function, an access function can be defined using options *:accessor* (read/write mode), *:reader* (read-only mode), *:writer* (write-only mode). Calling an access function defined in this way with an object as an argument we obtain the value of its appropriate instance variable.

Example
```
(defclass teacher () ( . . .
```

```
                              (children-number :initform 0
                                               :accessor
                                               num-of-children)
                         )
)
(setq susan (make-instance 'teacher))
(setf (num-of-children susan) 2)
```

The last option which can be used in instance variable description is
:allocation. Using this option we can describe (using *:allocation :instance*
default) whether we mean a variable which can have a different value for
each instance (i.e. an instance variable) or whether the value of this variable should be stored just once as part of the class description (using
:allocation :class) and shared by all instances (i.e. a class variable).

6.4.2 Generic functions

A generic function is a function which offers different executable codes
(called methods in CLOS) for different contexts of usage, i.e. a generic
function can be used with:

- Different types of arguments
- Different numbers of arguments.

The semantics depends on the context built by arguments. To allow the
different kinds of arguments, we define so many methods of the same
name for how many classes of objects to which it should be applicable.
  Methods defined in a class have to be mentioned in options of instance
variables which are used by them.

Example
```
(defclass circle () ((r :initarg :r :reader surface)
                     (x :initarg :xval)
                     (y :initarg :yval)
                     )
)
```

In a defmethod, required arguments are represented not only by a
symbol (as in defun) but by declaring the class of objects for which the
method is applicable. If the class name is t, the argument can be anything
(i.e. an instance of any class). The different numbers of arguments can be
achieved using optional arguments.
  There is also a defgeneric macro that can be used to declare a
specific generic function.

6.4.3 Methods in the class hierarchy

When using methods in a class hierarchy we may want a method to be inherited, to be shadowed, or some combination of both these concepts. When the name of a method is overloaded, i.e. when more than one method is applicable, then the one is invoked which has been defined in the closest environment of the object's class.

It can often be the case in class specialization that the specialized class uses a similar method and this similarity can be expressed as a composition of new functional features with an inherited method. In this case, we can use the function `call-next-method`, which invokes the next most specific method in the class hierarchy. The next most specific method can either inherit argument from the overloaded method (if `call-next-method` will be invoked without arguments) or can obtain an argument given in the `call-next-method` call.

We can also describe what should happen before applying the inherited method (using option *:before* to the function name) or after applying the inherited method (using option *:after* to the function name). When some methods with option *:around* are defined in the hierarchy, then all these methods (of the same name) will run first (most specific first), before *:before-methods* and *before methods* called by `call-next-method`. It is also possible to define a list of methods which should be invoked (*:method-combination*) and to invoke not the first but the last specific method from the most specific methods first.

The important question in all object-oriented systems is what happens with objects as class instances when the definition of their class is changed. In CLOS, all existing instances will be automatically updated to match the current, changed class definition.

6.5 PROGRAMMING IN AutoLISP

In the eighties the shortcomings of the relational model of DBMS were recognized in computer graphics. In commercial computer graphics systems there was a need to store figures in a CAD database. One of the producers, Autodesk Inc., used a tool named AutoLISP based on COMMON LISP for their product AutoCAD to support the additional extension by user-defined application oriented functions. AutoLISP is a small subset of COMMON LISP with some additional functions for figure processing that are specific to AutoCAD. Since AutoCAD can run on IBM PC-compatible machines it has become very popular. AutoCAD has an open architecture, i.e. it can be extended in the way the user needs for his or her own personal design. The possibility of using AutoLISP is the most powerful capability for extending AutoCAD. By writing programs in AutoLISP, new commands can be added to AutoCAD by using `defun` to define functions implementing those commands.

6.5.1 Storing figures

In AutoLISP, defined functions (`defun`) can be stored in a library and then loaded and executed by AutoCAD. The AutoCAD can pass a command line to AutoLISP for evaluation. In newly defined AutoLISP functions, the `command` function can be used to submit commands and data to AutoCAD.

Example

```
(defun drawl ()
        (command "pline" ........ a command of AutoCAD
            (setq x ())
        .
        .
        )
)
```

In this case, we feed the command "pline" to AutoCAD activating its `polyline` command.

Each figure part will be appended as an element of the association list representing the whole figure. A set of AutoLISP functions provides access to objects (in AutoCAD they are called *entities*). They can be selected and their values retrieved and modified. No functions are provided for creating entities directly. This will be done by AutoCAD commands.

The drawing system AutoCAD makes it possible to store the figure drawn in a list which is suitable for AutoLISP processing. Each part of the figure (it could be denoted as an object) is stored as an element of the a-list. There are special functions (`entnext, entlast, entget`, etc.) available for manipulation upon this list. Each figure part has a unique identifier supported and automatically generated by the system. This identifier and other attributes of the figure part are stored in a list which is accessible from the a-list. Each attribute has its key which is called a group code in AutoLISP (Fig. 6.4). The object identifier, called an entity name in AutoLISP, is a pointer into a file maintained by AutoCAD's Drawing Editor, from which AutoLISP can find the database record representing the object.

Example
Using a command

```
(setq a (entget (entlast)))
```

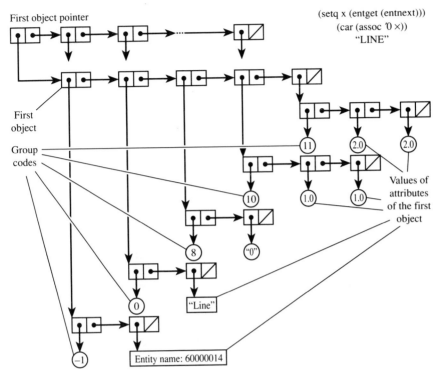

Figure 6.4 A figure and its parts stored in association lists

we obtain the object description of the last stored figure part. It can appear as follows:

The list representing the object description:

```
((-1 . <Entity name:6000008>) . . . unique identifier
(0 . "LINE") .................... type = a line
(10 1.0) ....... X-coordinate of the start point
(11 2.0) ....... X-coordinate of the end point
(20 1.5) ....... Y-coordinate of the start point
(21 3.5) ....... Y-coordinate of the end point
(30 5.0) ....... Z-coordinate of the start point
(31 6.5) ....... Z-coordinate of the end point
(62 1)   ....... the line will be drawn in red
)
```

The numbers −1, 0, 10, 11, 20, 21, 30, 31, 62 are group codes introducing attributes of the object.

There is a function `entnext` available which returns the name of the first object from the a-list when called without an argument, and the next object when called with an argument. The identifier of an object (a figure part) found by the function entnext will be used as an argument for the function entget which returns the list of properties associated with the given object. In AutoCAD it is an association list as described above.

Example

To process the complete association list of an AutoCAD figure the following template can be written:

```
(defun PROCFIGURE()
     (setq elem (entnext))
     (while elem
        (< . . . call of any processing function
         . . . > (entget elem))
         (setq elem (entnext elem))
     )
)
```

Using this, a function can be written which changes some attribute of all objects, e.g. all lines should be typed in bold.

Example
```
(defun BOLD ()
     (setq elem (entnext))
     (while elem
       (setq type
            (cdr (assoc 0 (entget elem))))
       (if (equal type "LINE")
            (< . . . processing of the found
            association list . . . >)
       )
            (setq elem (entnext elem))
     )
)
```

Using the method given in the example above, we can examine any condition of the attributes of any object in the association list. Such a query can be made flexible using function getstring.

Example
```
(setq typetobefound (getstring "\nEnter type:"))
```

Updating is supported by a function entmod which provides an object description in the format returned by entget, and updates the database information for the object whose name is specified by the object identifier (the group code −1 in the a-list). For modifying the elements of the object description, function subst will be used.

SEVEN

CONCEPTS OF OOP IN Smalltalk AND OPAL

The Smalltalk programming language is a uniformly object-oriented language and possesses all the features described in Chapter 4, e.g. all entities used in Smalltalk are objects. The concept of Smalltalk is based on objects, messages, classes, instances, and methods. To avoid an infinite regression of message sending, methods that do not send any messages but perform basic operations must be available. They are written in machine code and are called *primitive* methods. In general, users are not permitted to write these methods.

Programming in Smalltalk consists of creating classes (usually as specializations of existing library classes), creating objects as instances of classes, and specifying sequences of message exchanges among objects. An illustrative example is given in Fig. 7.1. The development of a Smalltalk program is supported by a very convenient graphical user interface.

The Smalltalk (we refer to Smalltalk-80) system includes:

- A set of classes representing the standard functionality of a programming language: arithmetic data structures, control structures, and input/output facilities.
- A set of classes representing more or less pure data structures (called collections). The common data structures of arrays and strings are provided by classes that have indices and external ordering corresponding to them.
- A set of classes that can be used to view and edit information. There are classes for representing and manipulating bitmap images, including bitmap images of fonts, classes for representing files as well as directories.

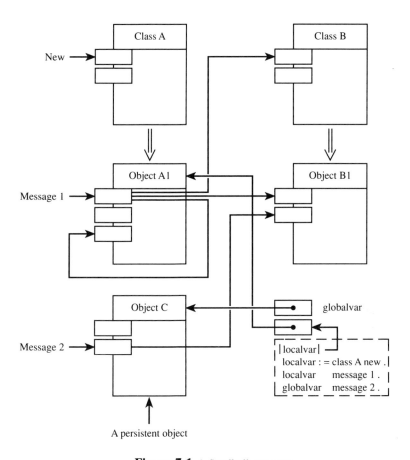

Figure 7.1 A Smalltalk program

The Smalltalk system includes the standard control structures (in the form of objects and messages) which can be found in most programming languages (*if . . . then . . . else, while*). Classes and instances are used as units for organizing and sharing information, and subclassing as a means of inheriting and refining existing capabilities.

In this chapter we will present only an introduction to Smalltalk. Since this book is about databases, we prefer to focus on the OPAL language which can be described as a database-oriented dialect of Smalltalk used in the commercial object-oriented DBMS GemStone (Bretl *et al.* 1989; *Programming in OPAL, 1989; TOPAZ–OPAL Programming Environment Manual*, 1989; *GemStone C++ Interface*, 1992). This database system will be employed in our examples.

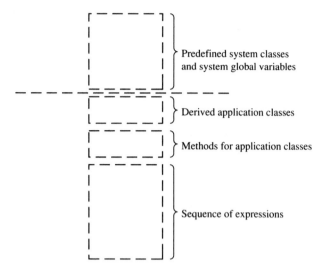

Figure 7.2 A Smalltalk program and its structure

7.1 THE STRUCTURE OF A Smalltalk PROGRAM

The structure of a Smalltalk program is shown in Fig. 7.2. We can usually distinguish the following main parts:

- A package of predefined library classes
- A package of subclasses derived by specialization from the predefined classes for the purposes of the current application
- Definitions of global variables
- Definitions of local variables
- Definitions of objects as class instances
- Sequence of messages
- Storing results into the global variables.

7.1.1 Expressions

In the Smalltalk syntax, expressions are the basic elements. When evaluated, they return an object. Among elementary Smalltalk objects we can find structures known from the procedure-oriented languages such as integers, strings, and arrays.

A Smalltalk expression can have one of the following four lexical forms: a literal, a variable, a message, and a block. Literals and variables will be shown using examples (all necessary details can be found in specialized books (e.g. Goldberg and Robson, 1983). In these examples we use the convention that local variable names begin with lower-case and global variable names with upper-case letters (the scope of variables will be discussed in Sec. 7.2.2).

7.1.2 Messages

A message consists of a receiver object, a message selector (i.e. the message name), and a list of arguments (can be empty). Three types of message exist:

- Unary messages (e.g. *2 sqrt*)
- Binary messages (e.g. *2 + 1*)
- keyword messages (e.g. *10 rem: 3*).

A *keyword* message has the following syntax:

```
<object name> <message name> : [<list of arg.>]
```

When composed, messages are evaluated from the left with decreasing priority from unary messages, keyword messages to binary messages. In response to a message the receiver returns an object (exactly stating its address) which becomes the value of the expression. An assignment expression has the following form:

```
Smalltalk              OPAL
<object> <- <value>    <object> := <value>
```

Messages can be chained in an abbreviated form when they have the same receiver:

```
Employees add: E1; add:E2.
```

which means

```
Employees add: E1.
Employees add: E2.
```

These are denoted as *cascading* messages.

7.1.3 Blocks

A block is an object that can execute an expression placed within its brackets if requested, i.e. if it receives the message value:. It is a sequence of expressions separated by the character '.'. It begins with the character

'[' and ends with a ']'. Evaluation of a block must be requested explicitly. It is possible to pass one or more arguments to a block before its execution. In a block, the arguments are specified at the beginning of the block by identifiers beginning with a colon ':'. Arguments are separated from expressions by the bar character '|'. Blocks are used in control structures.

Example
```
[:i :j | var1 <- i . var2 <-j ]
```

The arguments of a block are local variables to that block. To evaluate a block with an argument, the message value: *anArg* (or *valueWithArgs: anArray* for more arguments) must be sent with an argument that will be passed to the block.

7.1.4 Using control structures

Smalltalk uses the following three types of control structures (exactly— built-in methods providing this functionality are available):

- the loop (*like for, do*),
- the test (*like if . . . then . . . else*),
- the conditional loop (*like while, repeat*).

It does not use an equivalent to the case statement (not necessary—late binding can be used).

A loop can be constructed by sending a message do: to a collection of elements with a block as an argument.

```
<list> do: [ <block> ]
```

Example
```
| prod |              "a local variable declaration"
prod <- 1.
listInt   do:   [:eachInt | prod <- prod * eachInt]
```

This has the effect of calculating the product of all integers contained in the listInt (declared and used as a global variable somewhere else).

A test can be constructed by sending a message *ifTrue:, ifFalse:* to an object which has a Boolean value. A block has to be given as an argument of the message *ifTrue: or ifFalse:* which specifies what has to be done if the object's value is true or false.

Example
```
(anInt = 0) ifTrue: [outPrint <-'No use as a
                                 divisor']
```

The expression anInt = 0 means that a binary message '=' with an argument 0 has been sent to the objects anInt. It will be evaluated and the resulting object will receive the keyword message ifTrue: with the block [outPrint . . .] as an argument.

An equivalent of the *if . . . then . . . else* statement appears as follows:

```
(<an expression having Boolean value>) ifTrue:
                                  [ <block1> ]
                                          ifFalse:
                                  [<block2> ]
```

A conditional loop can be constructed by sending a message whileTrue: (or whileFalse:) to a block with another block as argument.

```
result <-
        [ <block1 having Boolean value> ]
             whileTrue:
        [ <block2 of actions, i.e., body of loop> ]
```

Block1 here is an object returned by a message which returns a boolean object (e.g. one of message >, <, =, etc.). As long as the condition (i.e. the value returned by the evaluation of the first block) is true, the second block is evaluated. When the evaluation of the first block returns false, the iteration stops. The result (i.e. the last evaluation of the block2) will be referenced by the variable result.

7.1.5 Object returned by a method

The name of a method is the same as that of the message to which the method must allow a response to be made. A method will be described by its name followed by a list of expressions separated by spaces (examples have been given in Sec. 6.5). When a method terminates, the receiver returns an object to the sender. The default object is the receiver itself. When it is required that another object be returned, this is indicated in the method by prefixing the object to be returned with the character '^'. As soon as this character is found, the object produced by the expression that follows is returned to the sender and the method terminates.

```
xPositive:x           "  .  .  .  name of the method"
(x > 0)   ifTrue:     [ ^true]   "returns true"
          ifFalse:    [ ^false]  "returns false"
```

abbreviated to

```
xPositive:x
              ^(x > 0)
```

Temporary variables can be declared in a method, but they are only accessible during execution of that method. To declare temporary variables their names must be placed between two '|' characters.

```
<name of the method>
   | <names of the temporary variables> |
   < list of expressions >
```

Often it is necessary that a message should examine the internal state of the receiver, i.e. a value of its instance variable. For this purpose, all methods have access to the special variables self, which represents the receiver. Using self we can invoke a receiver's method, and we can invoke the current method recursively.

Example
A method which returns an absolute value of a numerical receiver can be written as follows:

```
(self >= 0) ifTrue: [^self]
            ifFalse:[ ^0-self]
```

When a message is sent, an object receives it and searches in its class for a method that has the same selector as the message. If it does not find it, it continues its search in the superclass of its class. This process is continued throughout the sequence of its superclasses until the correct method is found. If the method has not been found at all, a run-time error has occurred.

There are many books available describing details of Smalltalk-80 (e.g. Goldberg and Robson, 1983) and Smalltalk/V. We will now describe the OPAL language. Most of the properties which we will describe in the OPAL environment are also available in Smalltalk, but occasionally the syntax is slightly different.

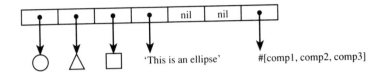

Figure 7.3 A heterogeneous array

7.2 PROGRAMMING IN THE OPAL LANGUAGE

The OPAL language was derived from Smalltalk-80 because of its lack of support for database applications, and in particular for the following reasons:

- Smalltalk is implemented as a single-user, memory-based, single-processor system.
- Large disk-based objects require new storage techniques. One of these objects may be too large to fit into main memory, and will have to be stored in a paged format.
- Algorithms used for hashing a set of objects in Smalltalk have been found inadequate for supporting large disk-oriented collections of data. Smalltalk hashes a set of elements by value, but in object-oriented databases we also need hashing by object identifiers.
- As a memory-based system, Smalltalk does not make it possible for the user or the database administrator to influence the physical storage management, i.e. to specify where a certain object should be stored. Smalltalk possesses no clustering tools.

7.2.1 Arrays

Arrays are heterogeneous and dynamic in OPAL. This means that objects stored in an array can be instances of different classes (Fig. 7.3). Physically, only pointers are stored in an array and the size of the array need not be given because an array is flexibly extendible. It brings overhead and therefore, where possible, the size of an array should be given for reasons of efficiency.

Example
In this example, we assign values of different types to variables and then assign these variables to the first three elements of a heterogeneous array.

```
| array1 var1String var2Char var3Number |

var1String := 'This is a string'.
```

```
var2Char      := $a.
var3Number    := 7.
array1        := Array new.
array1        := #[var1String, var2Char, var3Number].
```

The idea of heterogeneous array has also been used in systems dBASE and FoxBASE to enable a record to be stored in an array in such a way that one element of the array contain one item of a record.

7.2.2 Scope and visibility of variables

Variables are containers for objects in OPAL and Smalltalk. 'Types' of variables exist in OPAL; however, they distinguish the scope and visibility rather than the type of the value of the variable (Fig. 7.4). We can distinguish:

- Temporary variables
- Global variables
- Instance variables
- Class variables
- Pool variables.

Temporary variables are local in methods. They are declared by enclosing them in pairs of vertical bars (|) at the beginning of an expression series. It has been recommended that their names begin with a lower-case letter.

Global variables are systemwide objects and are not automatically removed after a program has been executed, i.e. they denote persistent objects. They are not confined to use in an expression. Global variable names have been recommended to begin with an upper-case letter. Each user has his or her own list of global names (*UserGlobals*).

Instance variables are defined in a class definition. They contain internal values of the object, are local in scope of each object and are accessible for updating only for the object's methods (accessible for reading also using dot notation, e.g. *anyTeacher.name*).

Class variables are defined in a class definition and are common for all instances of the class. They contain data common to all instances.

Pool variables may be defined in each class and enable any number of classes and their instances to share data, i.e. they may be defined common to all instances of all classes.

7.3 CLASS DEFINITION

Multiple inheritance is not supported in OPAL. Each class defined in OPAL is a direct or indirect subclass of a system class Object. This is

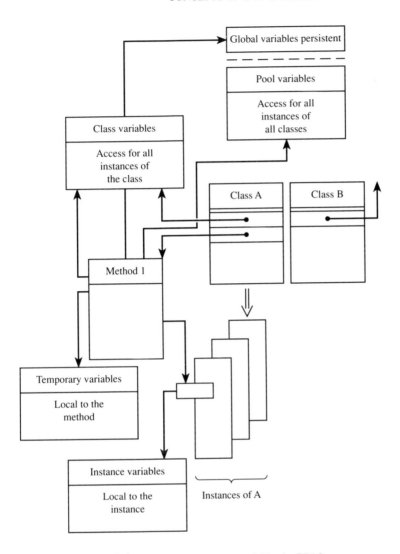

Figure 7.4 Scope and visibility of variables in OPAL

useful for inheritance of common properties of all classes, e.g. to answer the new message. OPAL uses the following syntax for defining classes:

```
<superclass> subclass : '<subclass name>'
    instVarNames : #(<list of instance variables>)
    classVars : #(<list of class variables>)
    poolDictionaries : #[<list of pool variables>]
    inDictionary : <where to look up global variables>
```

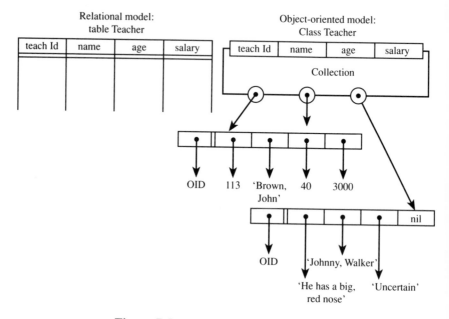

Figure 7.5 Defining a simple class in OPAL

```
constraints : #(<list of type constraints>)
isInvariant : <a flag of invariance>.
```

It is a common practice to construct a database as a set of records. Each record represents an entity and each field in a record an attribute. In OPAL an attribute will be represented by instance variables. Generally, attributes specify the individuality of each object, so they have to be stored in variables local in these objects.

Example
We describe again the database applied to university environment. In the first approach (Fig. 7.5) only instances of one class will be used. In relational database terminology, we would say that we define only one table, but here we must define the structure of an object as a tuple of containers (we can but we need not constrain the content of these containers) and we must distinguish between a class of objects and a class of collections where these objects can be stored.

```
Object subclass : 'Teacher'
```

```
instVarNames : #'teachId', 'name', 'age', 'salary')
classVars    : #()
poolDictionaries : #[]
inDictionary : UserGlobals
constraints  : #()
isInvariant  : false.
```

In this very simple example, we can follow the differences compared with SQL or dBASE where the type and the size of attributes (as components of the described object) had to be predefined at the time when the table was created (i.e. at compile-time) and attribute values are stored directly. There is an exception in Memo-fields in dBASE. This attribute contains a pointer into a .DBT-file, but this attribute cannot be used in querying.

7.4 THE PREDEFINED CLASS COLLECTION

The concept of re-usability in object-oriented programming is supported by powerful libraries which contain predefined classes for all purposes. It is not always easy for beginners to master all the available possibilities.

Class `Collection` is the superclass of all the collection classes. Collections are the basic structures used to store objects in groups in an organized manner. The most frequently used of these classes are:

- Array
- String
- Dictionary
- Bag
- Set

Any subclass in the class `Collection` generally provides the following capabilities to the user:

- Searching, adding, removing, accessing, and changing elements of a collection.
- Iterating over the elements of a collection by message do: to process all elements of a collection.

The class `Collection` and its subclasses are particularly important for database processing. In object-oriented database programming we use them in the same sense as we use files in dBASE and tables in SQL. The hierarchical structure of classes (important for this text) in OPAL is as follows:

```
Object
     Collection
          Bag
               Set
                    Dictionary
                              IdentityDictionary
                              SymbolDictionary
                                   LanguageDictionary
                         UserProfilSet
                         SymbolSet
                         SequenceableCollection
                    Array
                         InvariantArray
                         Repository
                         SymbolList
                    String
                         InvariantString
                              Symbol
               HashDictionary
                    IntegerHashDictionary
                    StringHashDictionary
                         SymbolHashDictionary
          CompiledMethod
          Magnitude
               Character
               DateTime
               Number
```

For creating a collection and inserting new elements into a collection, we can use the following messages:

- *new*.
- *withAll: aCollection*   It creates a new instance of the receiver containing all of the objects stored in *aCollection*.
- *add: object*.
- *addAll: aCollection*.

For testing, we can use the following messages:

- *includes: anObject*.
- *includesValues: anObject*.
- *isEmpty*.

- *occurrencesOf: anObject.*

For searching, we can use the following messages:

- *collect: aBlock.*
- *detect: aBlock.*
- *detect: aBlock ifNone: exceptionBlock.*
- *reject: aBlock.*
- *select: aBlock.*

7.4.1 Non-sequenceable collections

The non-sequenceable collections—represented by a bag as the most common of them—are unordered groups of objects. They are dynamic in the sense that they grow accommodating new objects. Unlike sets, they can contain several identical objects, i.e. one object in several occurrences. We get it by sending a message *add: anObject withOccurences: anInteger.*

The class Bag introduces a number of messages for removing objects:

- *remove: anObject.*
- *remove: anObject ifAbsent: exceptionBlock.*
- *removeAll: aCollection.*
- *removeAllPresent: aCollection.*

In this context, we mention the problem of *dangling pointers*. In Gem-Stone, it is solved in the following way. If we remove an object, we delete only the pointer to it. This pointer is implemented as an object identifier as will be explained in Chapter 10. There can be many pointers to one object. When all these pointers are deleted, the object will be automatically removed by the garbage collector. This means that the user cannot explicitly delete an object.

On bags and sets we can perform set operations such as union (a message +), intersection (a message *), and difference (a message −).

The class Dictionary makes possible access to the elements via keys. It retrieves objects with an external lookup key. Each element of a dictionary is an unordered bag of pairs (class Association) containing a key and data.

Example
In this example, we show how a dictionary will be created, assigned and retrieved.

```
| dict |
dict := Dictionary new.
```

```
"comment in OPAL - storing elements in the
 dictionary"
dict at: #key1 put: 'an explanation1'
dict at: #key2 put: 'an explanation2'
"retrieving elements from the dictionary"
dict at: #key1
```

The message at: can be used for storing and retrieving, but if, for example, 5 is used as a key then it does not mean that the fifth position in the underlying structure will be inserted or retrieved (it is a key, not an index). The message *includesKey: aKey* tests to see whether the receiver dictionary contains the given key.

7.4.2 Sequenceable collections

Objects as instances of subclasses of a sequenceable collection (an abstract class) can be referred to as array elements in procedure-oriented languages such as Pascal. The subclass `Array` is a typical representative of sequenceable collections.

There are a number of useful messages which can be sent to an instance of a sequenceable class:

- *atAllPut: anObject.*
- *first.*
- *last.*
- *indexOf: anObject.*
- *addLast: anObject.*
- *insert: aSequenceableCollection at: anIndex.*
- *deleteFrom: startIndex to:stopIndex.*
- *deleteObjectAt: anIndex.*
- *copyFrom: startIndex to: stopIndex.*

Example
Creating an array and assigning values to its elements will be written in the following way:

```
| morningDuties |
morningDuties := Array new.
morningDuties  at: 1 put: 'wake up';
               at: 2 put: 'really wake up'.
```

Message at: specified an index, *message put:* specified the data to be stored at the indexed variable. When creating an array, a method *new: size* can be used. Elements of an empty array will be initialized by nil. An array with its storage reserved previously will be processed more quickly.

Strings are represented by a specialized class String which describes a sequenceable collection of characters. They can be given as literals or created according to the definition above.

Example
```
| aString |
aString := String withAll: #($a $b $c).
```

The class String includes a number of useful methods such as:

- *findString: subString startingAt: startIndex.*
- *findPattern: aPattern startingAt: anIndex.*
- *matchPattern: aPattern.*

We will now interrupt our excursion into the OPAL classes. It would be too time consuming to name all the classes, including all the methods. As an example explaining a collection, we will continue with that given above.

Example
After having defined a class Teacher as

```
Object subclass : 'Teacher'
   instVarNames : #('teachId', 'name', 'age', 'salary')
   classVars    : #()
   poolDictionaries : #[]
   inDictionary : UserGlobals
   constraints  : #()
   isInvariant  : false.
```

we have to define a suitable collection class whose instance we will use for storing instances of Teacher. We start from a predefined class Set because it matches the reality.

```
Set subclass      :'SetOfTeachers'
   instVarNames : #()
   classVars    : #()
   poolDictionaries : #[]
   inDictionary : UserGlobals
   constraints  : #()
   isInvariant  : false.
```

These two definitions could be compared with those of a record and a file in a relational database system (e.g. in Datatrieve on PDP 11). They may be seen together as a table definition in SQL.

7.5 METHOD DEFINITION

We can define as many methods as we wish but at least we have to define methods for:

- Access to each instance variable which can be queried.
- Update of each instance variable which can be modified.
- Output of stored data.

For these purposes the methods will be divided into categories.

Example
```
category : 'Accessing'
    method : Teacher "Class name"
    name "Name of the method, no parameters"
            ^name
    %
```

The method can use the instance variables of the receiver. It returns the value of the instance variable name.

```
category : 'Updating'
    method : Teacher "Class name"
    name : aNameString "Name, one parameter"
            name := aNameString
    %
category : 'Formatting'
    method : Teacher
    asString
      (self teachId)+ ' ' +
      (self name)    + ' ' +
      (self age)     + ' ' +
      (self salary)
    %
```

A display method may not be that simple:

Example
All attributes of each object in the collection which contains all teachers will be stored in one line. Therefore, the following message sent to a set

of teachers will produce a table containing the appropriate strings.

```
category : 'Formatting'
method : SetOfTeachers
    asTable
        |aString|
        aString := String new.
        self do: [: n |
            aString := aString + n asString.
            aString := aString add: Character lf
                ].
        ^aString.
%
```

7.6 TYPE AND RANGE CONSTRAINTS

In a class definition, a type constraint for the named instance variables can be given. We will show this in the following example.

Example
Type constraints integrated in the class definition:

```
Object subclass  : 'Teacher'
    instVarNames : #('teachId', 'name', 'age', 'salary')
    classVars    : #()
    poolDictionaries : #[]
    inDictionary : UserGlobals
    constraints  : #[
                    #[#teachId, Integer],
                    #[#name, String],
                    #[#age, Integer],
                    #[#salary, Integer]
                    ]
    isInvariant : false.
```

Range constraints are applied before updating, i.e. they are given in updating methods.

Example
The following method contains a range constraint condition:

```
salary > 0
```

```
category :'Updating'
    method : Teacher      "Class name"
    salary : aSalary
```

This updates the receiver's instance variable salary only if the argument, aSalary, is positive.

```
(aSalary > 0) ifTrue: [salary := aSalary]
              ifFalse:[ ^'A salary cannot be
                          negative']
%
```

7.7 POPULATING A DATABASE

Populating a database means that some objects are created, supplied by data and stored in a persistent structure (see Sec. 7.8). Again, we will demonstrate with an example.

Example
We populate our database with two teachers:

```
| T1  T2  insertedTeachers |
T1 := (Teacher new) teachId: '113'
                    name    : 'Brown,John'
                    age     : '50'
                    salary : '2000'.
T2 := (Teacher new) teachId: '114'
                    name    : 'Crown,Frank'
                    age     : '40'
                    salary : '3000'.
```

New objects of class Teacher were created and initialized. They have to be stored in the SetOfTeachers structure. This structure will be created, populated and then stored.

```
insertedTeachers := SetOfTeachers new.
insertedTeachers add: T1; add: T2.
UserGlobals at: #AllTeachers
            put: insertedTeachers.
```

7.8 PERSISTENCE

All objects which are denoted by global variables have their persistent images. There is a persistent dictionary *UserGlobals* in an empty database (defined by the system). Also, all objects connected to any persistent object are persistent. Neither user nor programmer has to worry about that. In Chapter 10 the mechanism of object management will be described from the implementation point of view.

7.9 QUERYING IN OPAL

There are predefined messages suitable for searching in predefined classes like the class Set:

- *select: aBlock.*
- *reject: aBlock.*
- *detect: aBlock.*

Example
```
Query: Find all teachers younger than 40 with
       salaries over 3000.
   | foundTeachers |
foundTeachers := (UserGlobals at: #AllTeachers)
   select: [:aTeacher | aTeacher age < 40 &
                        salary > 3000]
```

The teachers found here can be displayed by sending the message asTable defined above. The variable foundTeachers contains a pointer to a subset of AllTeachers.

```
foundTeachers asTable.
```

7.10 INDEXING IN OPAL

In OPAL it is natural to represent a relation as a bag or set of objects. Each element corresponds to a record, and each instance variable of an element corresponds to a field. To make it easy to retrieve values from a record, one might define methods with names of instance variables in each class so that a receiver (an instance of that class) returns the value of the instance variable. To retrieve a value for read-only purposes can be made also by using the dot-notation. Using this, collections can be searched through in a relatively inefficient sequential manner.

To accelerate searching, indexing can be used. For this purpose, some constraints (Fig. 7.6) have to be introduced:

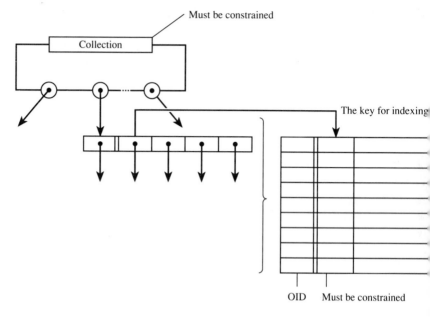

Figure 7.6 Contraints for indexing

- Only a constraint instance variable can be used as a key, i.e. the column in the virtual table of objects must be homogeneous.
- A collection to be indexed must contain only objects of one class (or its subclass) i.e. the collection must be homogeneous in the sense that all its objects contain the same constrained instance variable (direct defined or inherited).

Example
In the `teachId` attribute of the class `30Teacher`, only a value of type `Integer` is permitted.

```
Object subclass : 'Teacher'
  instVarNames   : #('teachId', 'name', 'age', 'salary'
  classVars      : #()
  poolDictionaries : #[]
  inDictionary   : UserGlobals
  constraints    : #[#[#teachId, Integer]]
  isInvariant    : false.
```

In the set subclass `SetOfTeachers`, only objects of the class `Teacher` are permitted.

```
Set subclass      : 'SetOfTeachers'
  instVarNames : #()
  classVars    : #()
  poolDictionaries : #[]
  inDictionary : UserGlobals
  constraints  : Teacher
  isInvariant  : false.
```

Two kind of indexes can be created:

- The identity index which supports identity queries, i.e. selects the elements of a collection in which some instance variable is identical to a target value (the comparing operator '==' will be used).
- The equality index which supports equality queries, i.e. selects the elements of a collection in which some instance variable has the same value but not necessarily the identical value as the target value (the comparing operator '=' will be used).

The identity index will be built on the objects of classes automatically by the system (object identity is supported in OPAL). The identity index can be built also on instance variables. In this case, we use a message `createIdentityIndexOn: nameOfInstanceVariable` (for creating an equality index we have to send the message `createEqualityIndexOn:`).

For atomic objects (characters, small integers), equality and identity are the same, and so creating an equality index effectively also creates an identity index. OPAL automatically uses the more efficient identity indexes even though an equality query has been given. In the process of creating an index to a nested instance variable, OPAL also creates identity indexes to the values that lie on the path to that variable.

Example
```
AllTeachers createIdentityIndexOn: 'teachId'
theTeacher := (UserGlobals at: #AllTeachers)
select: {:aTeacher | aTeacher.teachId == T177}.
```

This query is a identity query, and will be supported by the automatically produced identity index.

7.11 SORTING IN OPAL

Class Bag defines a mechanism to sort collection elements without message passing. Sort keys are specified as path, and they are restricted to paths that are able to bear equality indexes, i.e. which are constrained.

Although the paths given as keys must be fully constrained, they need not be indexed.

Example
```
sortedTeachers :=
AllTeachers sortAscending: 'name'
sortDescending: 'salary'.
```

A collection can be sorted on a composed key:

```
sortedTeachers :=
    AllTeachers sortAscending: #('age', 'name').
```

7.12 A SIMPLE APPLICATION

In Sec. 7.11 we described a primitive database comprising one table of teachers. Now we will increase the complexity of this example by appending new classes and by specialization of existing classes. This top-down method is suitable for explaining and teaching but not for the object-oriented design, where the bottom-up method is preferred. We will discuss this in Chapter 8. Of course, object-oriented databases are used typically for more complex problems (e.g. VLSI design, software design, etc.) but these problems are not suitable to be presented here.

7.12.1 Structured domain attributes

In this application we continue with the scholastic database by appending subjects as a structured domain attribute of the class Teacher (Fig. 7.7). We obtain a relation which is not in the 1. normal form.

This structure is only useful for showing a nested attribute representation in OPAL and how to initialize it.

Example
```
     | objectBrown   subSetOfSubjects |
objectBrown := (UserGlobals at: #AllTeachers)
   select: [:aTeacher | name = 'Brown,John'].
```

returns a pointer on the object found.

```
objectBrown.subject := #('algebra', 'calculus').
```
or
```
objectBrown.subject := #('algebra', 'calculus').
```

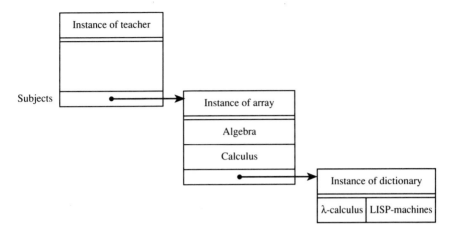

Figure 7.7 A nested attribute structure

or
```
subSetOfSubjects := Set new.
subSetOfSubjects add: 'algebra'; add: 'calculus'.
objectBrown.subjects := subSetOfSubjects.
```

7.12.2 A relationship

In the second approach we start from the sentence: 'Teachers teach subjects' and we append subjects as the next table. We know that there is a many-to-many relationship between Teachers and Subjects, and we will investigate how to describe relationships in object-oriented database systems (in this book represented by GemStone). First, we define the class Subject as follows:

```
Object subclass : 'Subject'
  instVarNames  : #('subjectId', 'name', 'descr')
  classVars     : #()
  poolDictionaries : #[]
  inDictionary  : UserGlobals
  constraints   : #[]
  isInvariant   : false.
```

To represent a relationship, we have two principal possibilities. We can use a table as in a relational model, or we can use a set of pointers as in a network model.

To represent a relationship as a table (Fig. 7.8) we define a new class

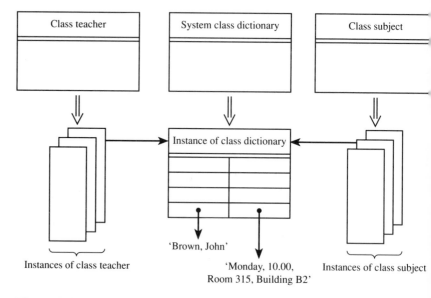

Figure 7.8 A relationship in an object-oriented database system represented by a table

`Teachers Activity`. This class will contain all data concerning each tuple <*teacher, subject*>. Each tuple will have a key part (identifying the tuple) and a value part. The most suitable representation using system classes will be the deriving of a subclass from the system class `HashDictionary`.

`HashDictionary subclass: 'TeachersActivity'`

To represent a relationship as a set of pointers (i.e. exactly as a set of object identifiers), we define a nested attribute subject in the class `Teacher` (Fig. 7.9) but we will not store strings describing subjects into it as in the previous example. We store pointers to instances of subjects there. These pointers will be organized in some of the subclasses of the system class `Collection`.

We will find the object representing the teacher John Brown in the persistent collection `AllTeachers`. The object found (i.e. the pointer to it) will be stored in the local variable `objectBrown`. Then we build a set of subjects which Mr Brown has to teach and we assign the pointer to this set to the instance variable `objectBrown.subjects`. Since the local variable `objectBrown` contains a pointer to the persistent object representing Brown's data, we have modified its instance variable subjects (initially set to nil).

`| objectBrown    subSetOfSubjects |`

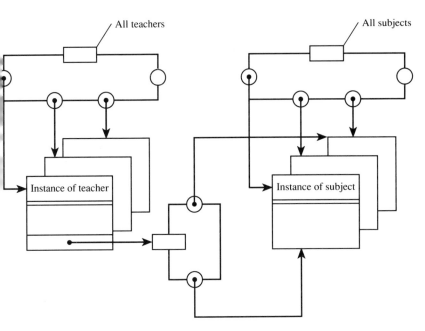

Figure 7.9 A relationship in an object-oriented database system presented by a network

```
objectBrown:= (UserGlobals at: #AllTeachers)
    select: [:aTeacher | name = 'Brown,John'].
subSetOfSubjects := (UserGlobals at: #AllSubjects)
    select: [:aSubject | name = 'calculus'].
objectBrown.subjects := subSetOfSubjects.
```

Using this structure, we can efficiently implement the query 'which are the subjects tought by John Brown'. We can only inefficiently answer the question 'who teaches Chemistry'. Therefore, we should add an instance variable 'teachers' in Subject.

The problem of referential integrity does not occur here, because if a subject does not exist we cannot obtain a pointer to it in the way described above.

We see that the relation represented as a table brings nothing new compared with the relational model. The relationship represented by two sets of object identifiers is a part of both objects involved in this relationship.

We will continue in our application by refining the environment. It is right that 'teachers teach subjects' but, more exactly, we can say 'teachers teach courses'. This describes an aggregation in the class environment because there is a *Is_part_of* relationship among courses and subjects. We can see that '*a_Teacher*' is a property of a course not of a subject. Since data structures are inherited and cannot be overriden, the definition of the class Subject must be changed.

In the class Subject, a class variable *responsibleTeacher* can be defined. This will contain a pointer to a teacher who is responsible for the whole subject, i.e. for all courses of this subject. To illustrate a *poolDictionary* variable, we introduce a head of department who is responsible for everything whose name is accessible from all instances of all classes.

Finally, we can add the student agenda. We define a class Student, we build a relation *Student_Course* as a collection of pointers to courses bound to each student and as a collection of pointers to students bound to each course.

7.13 A GemStone C INTERFACE

For certain database operations it can be preferable to use a C function rather than to perform an OPAL command. Very often, there are operations external to GemStone which use some predefined C libraries. The structure of GemStone is shown in Fig. 7.10. There are two possibilities for combining C and OPAL:

- To call C functions from within an OPAL method.
- To call an OPAL method and to access GemStone from a C program.

7.13.1 Using C functions in an OPAL method

The OPAL method invokes a user action routine written in C (Fig. 7.10) by sending a message *userAction*: to the System. The name of the C function called is given by *aSymbol*. (i.e. the name of the function preceded by '#'). The C function treats all objects as temporary objects. To make a newly created object a permanent part of the GemStone database it is necessary to return it as the function result and store it permanently by the OPAL mechanism.

The C function is, of course, prohibited to call some of the C functions incorporated into GemStone which would:

- Run the OPAL compiler or interpreter.
- Change the current database environment used by the invoked OPAL method.
- Interrupt the OPAL execution.

Example
```
    | tempArray |
tempArray := Array new: 10.
```

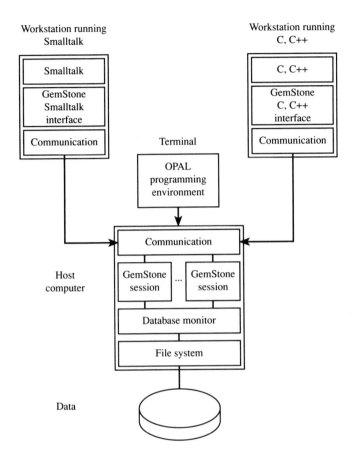

Figure 7.10 The structure of the GemStone database system

```
tempArray[1] := (UserGlobals at:#AllTeachers)
   select: [:aTeacher | 'teachId' = 113 ].
tempArray[2] := (UserGlobals at:#AllTeachers)
   select: [:aTeacher | 'name' = 'Smith,Frank'].
System userAction: #anyC_Action with: tempArray.
```

Once tested, the C application can be linked with the linkable version of the GemStone Interface C system to execute the C application as a set of object modules linked directly into the GemStone session process.

In the previous sections we used an access via OPAL commands without specifying the mechanism for offering these commands to GemStone. Now we can say that it is provided by an OPAL interpreter which is called TOPAZ. OPAL is proposed as a query language and does not include tools for programming user interfaces.

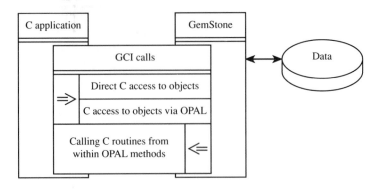

Figure 7.11 The GemStone C interface

7.13.2 Hybrid applications

As a hybrid application, we denote an application using the GemStone C Interface—GCI. This serves a C application and allows it to access data in the GemStone database from a C environment (Fig. 7.11) by:

- Offering interface C −> OPAL using the OPAL model for accessing data in the database.
- Offering a special C model for accessing data in the database.

For creating a hybrid application, the following steps are recommended:

- External interface of the application must be defined.
- It must be decided if it would be better to import the OPAL representation of objects into the C environment and to perform the operations there, or if only a message from the C environment into the OPAL environment should be sent to invoke an OPAL method for performing the operation.

7.13.3 C model for accessing objects in the GemStone database

Using this model, a representation of each object must be imported from GemStone into the C program before the C function is executed. GCI provides a powerful package of functions:

- For importing database objects from GemStone to C.
- For creating new database objects.
- For directly accessing and modifying the internal contents of objects (for elementary objects only).
- For exporting objects to the GemStone database.

The newly created or modified objects must be exposed to the GemStone database before it can commit the changes to the database.

There is a specialized C function for each purpose in the GCI. The list of these functions is very long. Advantages of this approach are:

- It is more efficient, particularly for computationally intensive portions of a database operation (no overhead).
- C library functions can be used.
- I/O functions for the user interface can be easily written.
- An interface to other software systems can be supported.

7.13.4 An OPAL model for accessing objects in the GemStone database

The GCI provides C functions for defining an OPAL method for a class, sending a message to an object, and compiling and executing fragments of OPAL code.

The C function *GciExecuteStr* sends a string containing OPAL code to GemStone for compilation and execution. It can be any self-contained unit of code that could be executed within a TOPAZ run command. Advantages of this approach are:

- The integrity of the data encapsulation is preserved.
- Functions in OPAL are more easily shared among multiple applications.
- Functions in OPAL are easier to implement.
- The overhead of transporting objects between C and OPAL is avoided.
- Predefined classes and methods may already exist in OPAL system classes which exhibit behaviour similar to that desired. By using them less effort will be required to implement a new function in OPAL.

7.14 A C++ INTERFACE FOR GemStone

By using the C interface for GemStone, OPAL objects can be created and manipulated by C functions but the database schema cannot be changed. The C++ interface (available for GemStone, Version 3.0) enables definition of C++ classes and storing these declarations in GemStone database schema.

The GemStone C++ Interface is based on single inheritance. Most GemStone's OPAL classes correspond to classes in a C++ interface library. All classes in this library are derived from the C++ class GS_Object. The GemStone C++ Interface exclusively uses special pointers to persistent classes called GPTRs (GemStone pointers) for manipulating objects. A parallel class hierarchy derived from GS_Object_GPTR provides each class with a corresponding GemStone pointer class.

The C++ class declarations (they must not include typedefs, structures, unions, enumerated types, or arrays with multiple dimensions) must be pre-processed and then stored in the database. This is provided by the GemStone C++ Interface utility which is called Registrar. In the pre-processing phase, the Registrar generates pointers _GPTR for all C++ classes stored in the GemStone database schema. A C++ class which should be storable in GemStone must be declared as a subclass of another persistent class. Its definition has to be divided into two files:

- Header file
- Code file.

The header file contains the declarations of classes (data structures and specification of member functions) and must include (*#include*) the GemStone class library, the Registrar-generated declaration file, the Registrar-generated in-line code. Each new class declaration must invoke the macro *GS_MEMBERS(class_name)* that declares some data access member functions whose code is supplied by the Registrar. The header file must also contain the specification of constructors and destructors because the default constructors provided by C++ compiler have not sufficient functionality to support the GemStone hierarchy.

The code file includes (*#include*) its header file and contains implementations (i.e., bodies) of member functions specified in the header file.

When a new class in C++ is created, it must be made known to GemStone by submitting it to the Registrar. The Registrar logs into GemStone, and creates and stores the new class declaration as a global persistent object in the appropriate symbol dictionary (*UserGlobals* is default). Then the Registrar generates code that enables accessing data in GemStone from a C++ program.

Every class declaration can contain so-called registered queries. A registered query is an OPAL-query (closed in *BEGINQ* and *ENDQ*) written inside comment brackets after the appropriate C function specification, i.e. it is a C member function specification with a body which consists of a comment. Registered queries are compiled by the Registrar, and the generated code is stored in the database. They can be used like any other member functions.

By using the GemStone C++ Interface one can combine the advantages of the C++ flexibility and the GemStone database capabilities (persistency, concurrency control, access control, etc.).

PART
THREE

DESIGN OF AN
OBJECT-ORIENTED DATABASE

EIGHT

ANALYSIS AND DESIGN METHODOLOGY

In Chapter 1 we stated that before building a database we need a model. Its purpose is

- To focus on important system features.
- To emphasize critical system features.
- To de-emphasize irrelevant system features.
- To build a platform for discussing changes and for refining and correcting the user requirements.
- To verify that the designer correctly understands the user environment.

The difficulty is to understand completely the problem domain and the role and the responsibility of the system to be designed.

When we specify the difference between analysis and design, we can briefly say that:

- Analysis builds a model and describes it in terms of the real modelled system.
- Design describes the same model in terms of the underlying software system.

Since the seventies, methods of structured analysis methodology based on functional decomposition of a system have been developed and published (e.g. Yourdon, 1989). In Sec. 8.7 we will present the dataflow diagram as a tool of this kind. The desired system is viewed as a set of processes whose inputs and outputs are defined. These processes are refined stepwise into sets of simpler processes until the primitive level is reached. It is a good starting point for designing a program as a system of modules and procedures, but there is little regard for the structure of the data and for the static semantic relations between data.

The entity–relationship diagram (as described in Sec. 1.4) used as a

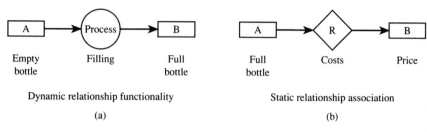

Dynamic relationship functionality

Static relationship association

(a)

(b)

Figure 8.1 Dynamic and static relationships

modelling tool in database technology is oriented on data structures and the relationships between them. The disadvantage is that the functional structure of a database cannot be expressed in an E–R diagram (Fig. 8.1). Often, the E–R model will be used in its modified and semantically enriched form which will be described as the extended entity relationship model (EER model). The concepts of inheritance (i.e. the specialization/generalization) and aggregation are its important additions to the E–R model.

In the object-oriented analysis we focus on contents of entities, not on the transformation of input to output. Each entity corresponds to a class in an object-oriented model. A survey of differences between the structured analysis and the object-oriented analysis can be concisely expressed in Table 8.1.

Table 8.1.

Difference	Structured analysis	OO analysis
Focused on	Transformations of input to output	Contents of entities
Starting point	Behaviour, process	Structures, objects
Functions are grouped together when they	Take part in the same process	Operate on the same object class
Analysis will be provided	Top-down based on specialization of functions	Bottom-up based on generalization of classes
Result is	Hierarchy of functions	Hierarchy of classes

The methodology of object-oriented database design is a topic of ongoing research and no unified, proved and widely used method exists today. Nevertheless, steps should be followed in the order:

- Initial problem statement
- Object identification
- Class identification
- Relationship modelling
- Class hierarchy identification
- Defining constraints
- Defining functionality
- Defining services
- Defining a schema of the desired object-oriented database.

These steps will be discussed in the following sections.

8.1 INITIAL PROBLEM STATEMENT

The analysis starts with specifying the purpose and features of the desired system. A description must be written which includes:

- Characteristic features of the system
- Expected goals
- Expected sets of queries
- Desired interface between the system and its users
- Technical aspects of design (hardware, software, team, time).

Functionality of the model must be separated into three groupings:

- Functions performed by the model, which manipulate data
- Functions performed by the user interface, which display the desired internal status of the system (e.g. selected data)
- Functions performed by the user interface, which enable the user to interact with the model.

This will be written in a natural language. From the description of the user interface we can recognize messages sent to the system from external objects (Fig. 8.2).

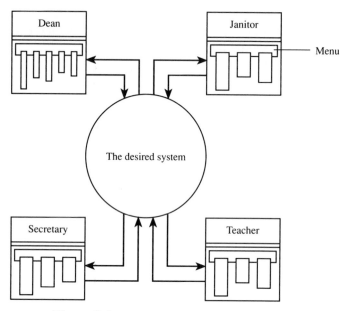

Figure 8.2 The desired system and user interfaces

8.2 OBJECT IDENTIFICATION

The initial elements of an object-oriented design are objects. The problem space can be viewed as a collection of objects and their methods. The problem is how to find them, or, more exactly, how to identify them. We will present the most popular approach to object identification here, namely:

• Grammatical inspection of documents describing the problem and the expected solution.

This method suggests that the designer starts with a natural language description of the desired system. This description must be written by someone who has experience in describing systems to be designed in natural language. To obtain a description expressing exactly what we have and what we need is the most important aspect of the analysis. Very often the description has to be repeatedly read and corrected by both the client and the designer.

In the method of grammatical inspection of documents, the fact is used that nouns describe objects and subjects (i.e. objects of the real world) in a sentence whereas verbs describe activities of these objects (i.e. activities invoked after accepting a message).

Example
```
Description: A cat is running after a mouse.
Objects: Cat, Mouse.
Methods: Hunt-method for the object cat.
```

This means that a mouse invoked a hunt-method in the cat.

Therefore all nouns will be found and used as potential identifiers of objects, and all verbs found will be used as potential identifiers of methods or relationships.

Example
```
Description: A teacher teaches a course.
Objects: Teacher, Course.
Relationship (i.e. association relation):
Teaches: tuples <teacher, course>.
```

The semantics of the verb in this sentence differ from that in the previous example. It identifies a relationship. Concerning this description, the cardinality of the relationship should be discussed:

- Could it happen that a teacher does not teach any course?
- Could it happen that a teacher teaches more than one course?
- What about the inverse relationship? Could a course be taught by more than one teacher?

Some designers distinguish two layers, two kinds of objects:

- User interface objects (transparent to the user)
- Application objects (not transparent to the user).

Very often an object represents a class of objects, because when we say 'A teacher teaches a course' we consider the teacher as a data type and the course as a data type. This sentence concerns classes. When we say 'Mr Brown teaches course of algebra No. 22' then this sentence concerns objects. We mention this because it depends on the description whether we discover objects or classes.

This nouns and verbs approach can be used as a starting point, but it can happen that objects will be used in the final version of the system which cannot be derived from the initial document in natural language, because their existence has been derived by clever factoring of the problem and by an abstraction. They can represent, for example, some dispatcher functionality units whose necessity would not be known until the analysis is finished. Some activities defined in verbs can be delegated to an abstract object in the model space which has no counterpart in the problem space.

Example
Real numbers are a very clever abstraction. In the real world (and also inside computers) there is nothing comparable to them. For example, we cannot cut a board of exact length of $\sqrt{2}$.

Summarizing, we see that objects can be identified in the first step by:

- Grammatical inspection of the description
- Abstraction.

8.3 CLASS IDENTIFICATION

After objects have been found and defined, we must specify their attributes and separate instances of different classes. Objects with a common structure and common behaviour should be defined as instances of one class. When specifying attributes of objects we focus on important system features.

Example
Which properties of teachers and courses will be included in our model depends on expected queries. If we expect that someone will be interested in querying the number of left-handed persons among teachers, we need to append this attribute to our model.

A list of all properties of all objects found in the description can be written and then it can be recognized which properties can be specified as attributes for distinct objects (Table 8.2). Objects having the same set of properties can be instances of one class (Fig. 8.3).

Table 8.2

Name	Description	Operating-System	Voltage	Colour
C	Compiler	UNIX		
QUICKBasic	Compiler	MS-DOS 3.3		
EIZO	Monitor		220	White
NeXT	Computer		110	Black

After looking for common properties of objects we examine their attributes, which can be primitive types like INTEGER as well as composite objects. This is the second source of our class-identification process. Observing composite objects, we obtain new space for object identification and a nested attribute hierarchy structure representing the relation '*Is_part_of*'. The composite object arguments of all identified classes should be decomposed at one level before proceeding to the next.

This assigning objects and classes is only preliminary at this stage of

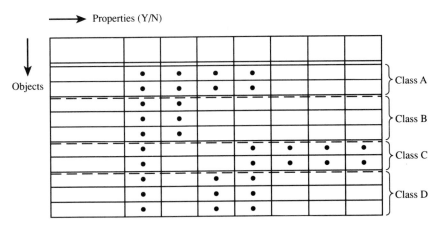

Figure 8.3 Class identification

design. The structure can be changed more times during the design process. There can be properties which we have forgotten or which the user has forgotten to tell us, there can be classes with the same data structure but different methods. These classes can be distinguished after defining functionality (Sec. 8.7).

8.4 RELATIONSHIP MODELLING

Relationships model the semantic relations among objects (Fig. 8.4). Relationships expressing the static semantics have to be identified and described in E–R diagrams. For creating a schema of an object-oriented database we emphasize the following relations among classes:

- Association—related objects build a tuple which have a semantic meaning and can have some common properties (e.g. a teacher teaches a course, a common property of the tuple is time and room). It will be shown that the association will be modelled as a set of object identifiers building a part of each object of the association.
- Specialization/generalization—(*Is_a* relationship). This may be modelled using the class hierarchy of inheritance.
- Aggregation—(*Is_part_of* relationship). This may be modelled using a class hierarchy of nested attributes.
- Message-flow structure (cross-references of messages). Following this relationship we can prove whether the functionality is complete in the sense that there is a receiver for every message sent.

Specialization and aggregation build class hierarchies which have to be identified.

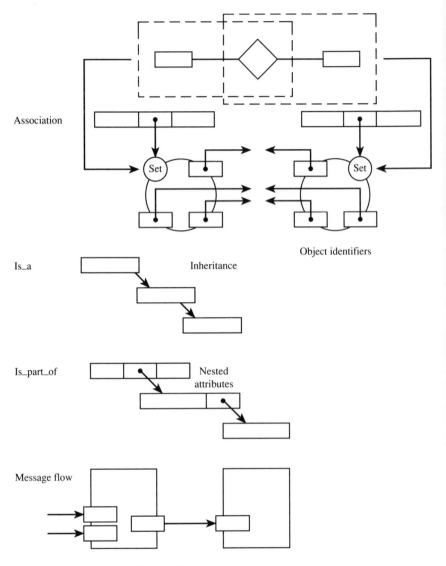

Figure 8.4 Relationship modelling

8.5 CLASS HIERARCHY IDENTIFICATION

The next step in object-oriented design is the design of the class hierarchy. This may be identified using generalization, i.e. we investigate groups of classes for their common structures. We try to get the maximal profit from the inheritance principle. The design process is often incremental. After obtaining a superclass by generalization we try to derive some suitable subclasses by specialization. The generalization and specialization are two faces of the relationship '*Is_a*'. Recognizing this, we obtain the class hierarchy of inheritance. Another kind of relationship which has to be recognized and identified is the '*Is_part_of*' relationship among classes.

This brings us the class hierarchy of nested attributes for complex objects. The design of the class hierarchy often needs to be reworked several times until the classes are easy to distinguish. We can distinguish between application-oriented classes (e.g. Course) and system-oriented classes (e.g. Set). These frequently used system oriented classes are part of the libraries of OODBMSs.

Usually, designers start from library classes and from the set of identified classes, and try to formulate the system of identified classes in such a way that it uses the predefined classes to the highest possible extent. For these purposes, the designer must master the predefined classes (of which there can be about one hundred to three hundred).

The last step in the class hierarchy abstraction is a design of an application-specific generic library which contains classes suitable for a specialization.

8.6 DEFINING CONSTRAINTS

Each of the defined classes has attributes which are usually constraints. Therefore, a part of the class design is the design of constraints. The problems with referential constraints, which occur in relational databases, are caused by dispersing objects in many tables and therefore they do not occur in object-oriented DBMSs.

8.7 DEFINING FUNCTIONALITY

The functionality of the desired system can be described by a dataflow diagram. A dataflow diagram (Yourdon, 1989) is a modelling tool used for describing the desired system as a set of transformations of inputs to outputs. It consists of:

- Processes which represent individual functions carried out in the system (denoted by circles).
- Dataflows which represent the transfer of information (its meaning can be used to name the arrow) from the output of one process to the input of another (denoted by arrows).
- Data stores which represent collections of data stored for the next use (denoted by two parallel lines).

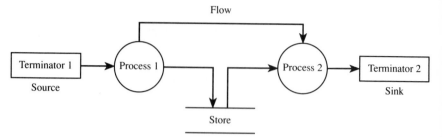

Figure 8.5 A dataflow diagram

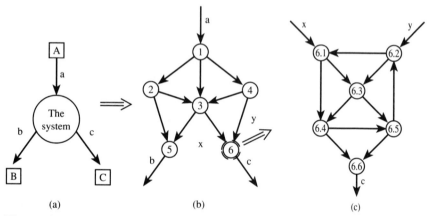

Figure 8.6 Levels in dataflow diagrams (a) Level 0 context diagram; (b) Level 1; (c) Level 2

- Sources which represent objects producing data (denoted by rectangles).
- Sinks which represent objects consuming data (denoted by rectangles).

The sources and sinks represent the interface between the system and the outside world (they are also called *terminators*), and their number and structure is fixed and cannot be changed. Dataflow diagrams (Fig. 8.5) are graduated according the level of abstraction. The diagram representing the top level of this hierarchy is called a context diagram (Fig. 8.6) and consists of one process and all terminators. It defines the interface of the proposed system (as a process) with the outside world. This process will be decomposed to obtain dataflow diagrams of lower level each with no more than about five to ten processes. Simple systems have about two or three levels, complex systems can have five to eight. This process represents expanding nodes of a graph and it is obvious that the number of inputs and outputs of an expanded node must correspond with those of the corresponding lower-level dataflow diagram.

As a starting point for functionality identification of the object-oriented system components we can use the dataflow diagram obtained

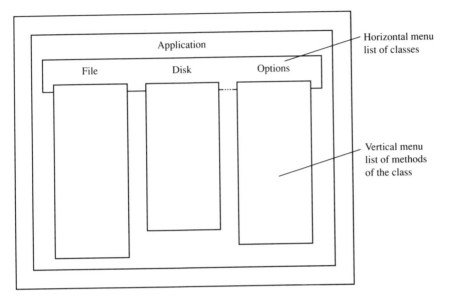

Figure 8.7 Menu of an application

from the grammatical inspection. Each element (except dataflow arrows, of course) of this diagram can be an object. We can write a list of objects extracted from the dataflow diagram in this way and compare it with the list of objects which can be created using identified classes.

In the next step of the design we can add methods identified from the dataflow diagram to classes representing objects. The structure of the classes will very probably change. It is necessary to identify common methods and remove them to a superclass. If some method often needs to be overridden it should be eliminated from the superclass. The relationship between a subclass and a superclass should be a specialization, which means that a subclass inherits all methods from the superclass and adds new methods of its own.

Example
An object in a model can represent an object from the problem space but it can also represent a group of methods (Fig. 8.7) which have a common environment and a common program to call them.

The objects found can be divided into active objects (represented by processes in the dataflow diagram) and passive objects (the remaining objects). Passive objects receive messages and provide the requested actions, active objects also send messages. In Booch (1991) we can read the following classification of objects:

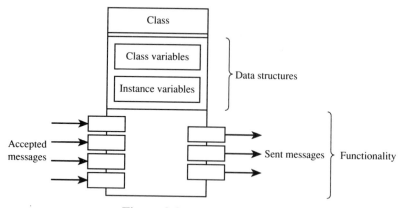

Figure 8.8 Class representation

- *Actor* an object which is only able to send messages.
- *Server* an object which is only able to accept messages.
- *Agents* an object which is able to both send and accept messages (Fig. 8.8).

There are no strict rules for identifying classes but there are some recommendations and hints from experienced practitioners:

- Entities in the problem space should correspond with classes in the model space.
- Methods should be single purpose.
- Methods should not be extended; when necessary, a new method should be defined.
- A method definition should not have more lines than the screen.

8.8 DEFINING SERVICES

The last step in one loop of the iteration when designing an object-oriented system is the defining of services, i.e. the functionality which is hidden in the mechanism of sending messages and invoking methods. When the functionality of classes was defined, methods were declared but not completely defined. In this step the algorithms offered by the methods have to be defined. For all classes, it is necessary to check whether there are senders and receivers for all defined messages and how the proposed mechanism is matching.

8.9 DEVELOPMENT OF THE SCHEMA OF AN OBJECT-ORIENTED DATABASE

In Fig. 8.9 we see the stepwise development and refinement of our knowledge about the desired system represented by a schema. In practice, it

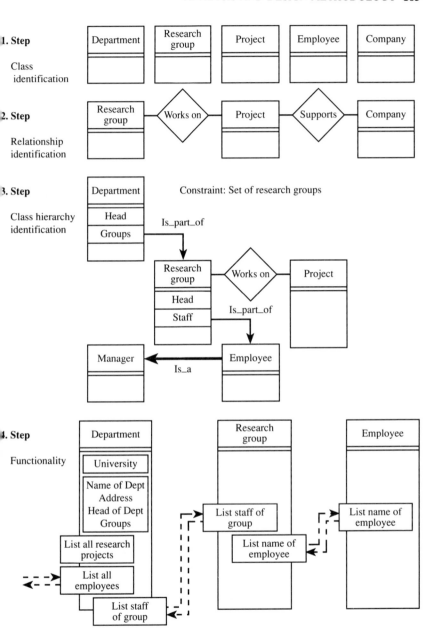

Figure 8.9 A stepwise development of a schema

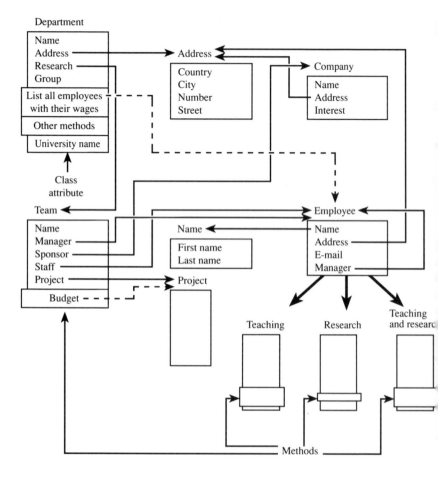

Figure 8.10 A schema of an object-oriented database

must be possible to choose the appropriate level of abstraction when using a schema, e.g. without functionality or without the message-flow structure. The complete schema can be very intricate even for simple applications.

An object-oriented database schema can be represented as a graph. In Fig. 8.10 classes as nodes are denoted by boxes. A class node contains the names of all instance variables, class variables, methods, and any messages which can be sent.

Nodes can be connected by three types of arc:

- A normal arc (that is, not bold and not hatched) indicates the class hierarchy of nested attributes (i.e. *Is_part_of* relation).
- A bold arc indicates the class hierarchy of inheritance (i.e. *Is_a* or superclass–subclass relation).

- A hatched arc indicates the send/receive message relation. We distinguish between messages expecting a response and those not expecting a response, i.e. we distinguish cases where the method is a procedure or a function. There are many other possibilities, e.g. to represent input parameters and results for methods, but there is a danger of destroying an easy survey.

8.10 RELATIONAL VERSUS OBJECT-ORIENTED MODEL

The major goal of object-oriented data models is to provide mechanisms for behavioural abstraction. Therefore they are similar to programming languages.

The relational model differs from an object-oriented data model in that it does not provide the possibility of directly modelling complex objects, and of defining inheritance relationships among sets of entities. Furthermore, it does not provide mechanisms to associate object behaviours with object definitions at schema level, since attribute domains can only be primitive domains in the relational model, and the object data structures are often dispersed into many tables. The semantics of object behaviour are dispersed among the application programs. Finally, object identity independent of the object status is not supported. Nested relational models overcome only the first of these limitations in that they allow the definition of complex objects but lack inheritance, object identity, and computational completeness.

The OODBMSs share many characteristics with OOPLs. In fact, some OODBMSs were defined starting from existing OOPLs (e.g. GemStone was defined from Smalltalk). An OODBMS, however, differs from an OOPL in that its objective is to manage efficiently a large amount of persistent, reliable, and shared data and to provide declarative primitives for data access and manipulation (that is, a query language).

NINE

DEVELOPING AN APPLICATION

There are two ways to develop an application solving an object-oriented database problem. First, let us assume that a commercially produced OODBMS can be bought. In this case there is the question of how to use it. From previous chapters it is obvious that primarily a model must be built. In this model we try to use the predefined classes to the greatest possible extent, i.e. if we choose, we prefer instances of predefined classes and we organize the system in such a way that it also can use the messages of the predefined classes. It should be more or less straightforward to map such a model into DDL, DML and DCL of the underlying OODBMS.

Second, since it can be difficult or almost impossible to obtain a commercially produced OODBMS for some computer systems, a program should be written (e.g. in C++) which will perform some functions of an OODBMS. In this case an efficient, problem-tailored system can be obtained, but there are some problems with:

- Storage-persistent objects because object-oriented programming languages do not support it (such as C++) or do not support it efficiently enough (such as Smalltalk).
- Transaction processing in a multi-user environment.

In this chapter we describe the first possibility. Details concerning implementation will be given in Chapters 10–12. As emphasized in Chapter 8, the methodology of object-oriented database technology is in its pioneering stage. In that chapter we introduced a recommended order of steps and some hints. In this we present a simple, illustrative case study. We will omit some details which are not important to our discussion here.

9.1 A COMPANY DATABASE

The principles described in Chapter 8 will be outlined here. We will design a small company database to illustrate the following necessary steps:

- Initial problem statement
- Object identification
- Class identification
- Relationships identification and modelling
- Class hierarchy identification
- Defining constraints
- Defining functionality
- Defining services
- Schema of the object-oriented database.

It is worth noting that a detailed description of such a small company database, including analysis of possibilities, would occupy an entire book.

9.2 INITIAL PROBLEM STATEMENT

A software system should be developed which will process:

- An inventory agenda
- A sale and purchase agenda
- A personnel agenda.

```
Description of the inventory agenda: . . .
Description of the sale and purchase agenda: . . .
Description of the personnel agenda: . . .
```

At this point, we have to include a specification of the high-level goal of the desired system, e.g. 'The purpose of the system is to help the clerk to find any data about items, suppliers, customers, and employees. This system consists of . . . '. Further, we should specify technical aspects of the solution, including high-level constraints, which include:

- Implementation constraints, e.g. the system should be implemented in GemStone on SUN workstations.
- Performance constraints, e.g. the response of the system must not exceed 1 minute.
- Resource constraints, e.g. the system must be developed by two people in two weeks.

The description of the agenda must contain not only a description of real-world objects (e.g. an invoice) and the way they are processed but also all abstractions and aggregations used in the existing processing (e.g.

groups of invoices for 1 month, 3 months, 6 months, 1 year). The description of the processing must also contain a description for all administrative procedures required (e.g. there is a procedure which produces a sum of all amounts of money of invoices received in a given quarter).

9.3 OBJECT IDENTIFICATION

The method of grammatical inspection of documents can be used here. From the description of the agendas we obtain:

- Objects: item, invoice, order, supplier, customer, employee, salesperson, purchaser, bookkeeper, group of all items produced, group of all invoices received in the given months, group of all orders sent in given months, etc.
- Activities: A supplier delivers items and sends invoices. A customer sends orders, obtains items and invoices, and pays invoices for items. A salesperson organizes sales to customers, and obtains a commission from invoices paid by customers. A purchaser organizes purchases from suppliers. A bookkeeper uses a survey of all invoices paid in the previous months, etc.

The task of identifying objects is often non-trivial, but this is not the case in this example because the agendas mentioned have been known for a hundred years (or rather, perhaps two thousand). There is a record about everything that is known about an object (in the handwritten documents for processing this agenda).

As the next step, we shall construct a context dataflow diagram (Fig. 9.1) and an E–R diagram (Fig. 9.2 on page 172).

9.4 CLASS IDENTIFICATION

In the example given, we can assume that each object identified represents a class, i.e. the initial problem statement was written in such a way that nouns in the textual description denote classes. As is often the case, when we write 'a supplier' we mean 'any supplier as a representative of this kind of object'. Classes found include:

```
Customer, Employee, Supplier, Salesperson, Purchaser,
Item, Invoice, Order, . . .
```

If there is an item in the description of a class that does not fit in any class

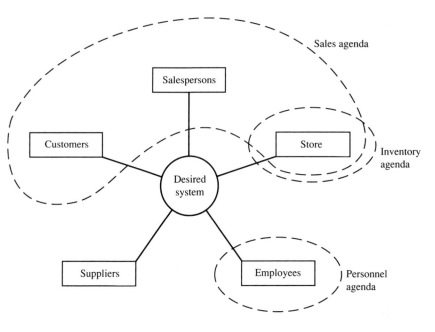

Figure 9.1 A context dataflow diagram - level 0

we have defined so far (or to any predefined class), we can assume that it should be put into a new class.

9.5 CLASS HIERARCHY IDENTIFICATION

To identify the class hierarchy, we follow the relationship *Is_a*, in the sense that we group together classes having some common attributes.

```
Customer
    Attributes:
      Name
      Address
      OrderingHistory
      ShipmentsHistory
      MailingHistory
      IsBuyingItems
      CouldBuyItems
Supplier
    Attributes:
      Name
```

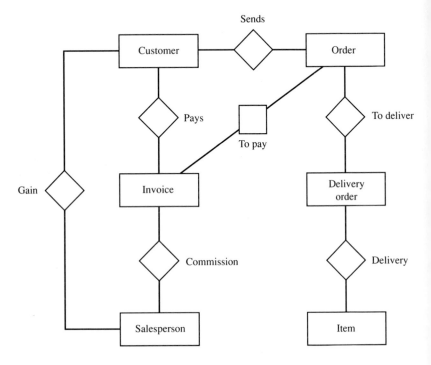

Figure 9.2 An E-R diagram of a simple sales agenda

```
      Address
      SalesHistory
      IsSupplyingItems
      CouldSupplyItems
Employee
   Attributes:
      PersNumber
      Name
      Address
      WorkingAs
      SalaryHistory
      TaxInfo
      EmploymentHistory
Item
   Attributes:
      CodeIt
      QuantityOnHand
      Price
      Description
SalesPerson
```

```
Attributes:
    all attributes of Employee + Turnover + Region
Purchaser
    Attributes:
    all attributes of Employee + IndexPrice
```

The class SalesPerson is a specialized class derived from Employee with appended attributes Turnover and Region. The class Purchaser is a specialized class derived from Employee with the appended attribute IndexPrice. All classes (except Item) have common attributes Name, Address. Therefore, we define a new class Heading as their superclass which contains attributes Name and Address.

```
Heading
    Name
    Address
```

This class will not be derived by the grammatical inspection from the initial statement but by generalization of existing classes. Usually we think that the attribute Name is a string but it can be a more complex structure.

Example: *Name as a structure*
Suppose that our company employs some Chinese staff whose names can be written as strings in a phonetic transcription but the company will also have these names in their pictorial form. One of these employees will lead the branch in Taiwan and the company will use the pictorial form of his or her name when sending letters.

Example: *Address as a structure*
In the modern world the address is more than a postal address. There can be included a phone number, fax number, telex number, or E-mail address. By building a single uniform address class, the burden of managing these differences has been shifted from the Heading class to the Address class, where it belongs. When writing a letter to a friend living in our town, we do not need to mention our international and regional prefix for the telephone number. Depending on how much our address and that of our friend differ, the telephone number can be automatically expanded.

```
Address
    TitleIfAny
    LastName
    FirstName
    SecondName
```

```
Street
HouseNumber
Town
ZIP
Country
LocalPhoneNumber
LocalFaxNumber
```

From the above examples it follows that when writing a letter to a customer we can use different components of objects `Name` and `Address`. In the next example we will show that some details of objects can be hidden.

Example
The attribute `Price of Item` is a common property, but there is nothing said about units of quantity. These units of quantity can be pieces or litres. This is a problem of the method which will be used for answering a message asking the price.

It can very easily happen that we can disclose (i.e. identify) new classes when defining attributes of the specified classes. First, we look up value-based attributes whose domains are integers, strings, etc. Second, we look up nested attributes such as arrays, records, lists, etc. In this case we have to disclose the relationship *Is_part_of*.

Some of the characteristics of an object can be represented in complex data structures. The searching in these internal data structures is performed by the object itself. This follows from the encapsulation concept. All other objects are found by sending messages.

Example
In the class `Item` there is the attribute `Price`. In examples this is an integer. In practice, it is not an integer but it is a complex structure representing dependencies upon the price of the product, the size of the delivery, and other aspects of the contract. Sometimes the customer and the supplier are supplying to each other. Then the sale contract can contain a condition that company A as a customer will buy our product X for price P if our company as a customer will buy product Y from the company A as a supplier for price Q.

In the implementation we use a price method which represents an algorithm accessing internal structures of the item. It can send messages asking details of contracts with particular customers or suppliers. In a simple case, there will be only a table specifying:

- 1 item . . . 5
- 10 items . . . 48

- 100 items . . . 400
- More than 1000 . . . call for price.

The refinement of semantics of the class attributes can bring new classes.

Example
In simple examples introducing the relational model the attribute `Salary` is always a number. In practice, it is a special case of a `Salary` called a `FixedSalary` but some employees get an `HourlySalary`. For some professions the algorithms for computation of the salary are non-trivial. We define a class `Salary` and its subclasses `HourlySalary` and `FixedSalary`.

```
Salary
      ClassificationClass
HourlySalary
      standardHoursRate
      overtimeRate
FixedSalary
      howMuch
```

A newly derived class must contain all the data structures of the super-class. Data structures cannot be overriden. If we were able to prove that our new, derived class does not contain at least one of the elements of its base, parent class (superclass), then we would have a clear indication that either there is something wrong with the definition of the superclass or that our new class is not really derived from this superclass. As shown in Chapter 7, an important concept of object-oriented design is a collection. This object serves to group other objects together, so that they can be referred to as a single entity. In database applications we often need an indexed collection (in GemStone we will find a predefined class called a `SequenceableCollection`). This is a collection with a searching mechanism using a key index. We know that not all collections are necessarily indexed, some may be viewed simply as buckets into which we store a number of distinct objects.

Example
In many classes we have used an attribute representing a history of development. This is a collection of facts over time. It is indexed, keyed by dates. If there are more items having the same date, we have to define our own internal keying scheme. It can be a combination of date and the order of facts from that date.

OrderingHistory	is a collection of customer's orders indexed by date and by orderNumber.
ShipmentsHistory	is a collection of the company's deliveries to the customers and it is indexed by date, by orderNumber, and by shipmentNumber.

9.6 DEFINITION OF CONSTRAINTS

We can write type constraints on attributes where we insist on single-type value (in the class definitions in GemStone), range constraints which prevent an incorrect updating attribute (in the updating methods in GemStone), and type constraints concerning indexing for indexed collections.

Example
Definition of type constraints in GemStone:

```
Object subclass 'Item'
        instVarNames : #('codeIt', 'quantOnHand',
                         'price', 'description')
            .
            .
            .
        constraints: #[#[#codeIt, integer],
                       [#quantityOnHand, integer]
                       ]
```

For indexing it is necessary to constrain the key (i.e. the pointer stored in codeIt can only point to an integer) and the element of the collection (i.e. only Items allowed).

```
SequenceableCollection subclass 'AllItems'
            .
            .
            .
        constraints: Item
```

9.7 DEFINING FUNCTIONALITY AND SERVICES

For defining functionality we use the dataflow diagram method shown here. In Fig. 9.3 we see a model of a simple sales agenda. It is obvious that the survey may be destroyed. In defining functionality we must distinguish between the system level and the application level.

Example
Appending a new order to a collection of orders is a system capability, as it is likely to be used in many applications. Before writing it we must investigate the predefined messages. Determining if a string represents a legal inventory part number code is an application capability, bound to the semantics of the application.

Usually, we will initially know data structures when dealing with an application's classes and we will use functionality of predefined system

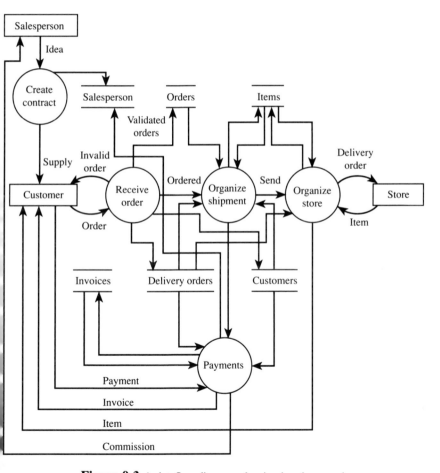

Figure 9.3 A dataflow diagram of a simple sales agenda

classes. For indexed collections (a `SequenceableCollection` in GemStone), the following messages are available.

- For accessing: first, last
- For adding: add: *newObject*, insert: *aSequenceableCollection at: anIndex*
- For manipulating: do: *aBlock, reverseDo: aBlock*
- For removing: *deleteFrom: startIndex to: stopIndex, deleteObjectAt: anIndex*
- For searching: *findFirst: aBlock, findLast: aBlock, indexOf: anObject*
- For updating: *atAllPut: anObject.*

The functionality on the application level will bring us the need for the following messages:

```
Item
  public:
     partNum:
     onHand:
     priceInfo:
     description:
  private:
     setPartNum:
     setQuantity:
     setPriceInfo:
     setDescription:
Supplier
  public:
     name:
     address:
     supplies:
     canSupply:
     is_SuppliedBy:
private:
     .
     .
     .

Customer
  public:
     name:
     address:
     buys:
     couldBuy:
  private:
```

.

.

.

```
Salary
   public:
      grossPay(hours)
      FixedEmployeeSalary
```

For `FixedEmployeeSalary` there is no computation (only an assignment). It makes it possible to send a message `grossPay(hours)` to the object `EmployeeSalary`. External objects will be able to send the same message to both hourly and fixed salary objects. This is just another case where a design decision has been made that keeps the system uniform, instead of providing many special cases. In cases such as this it is preferable to add a little overhead to one routine in order to make it conform to related routines, rather than to cause a host of different calling mechanisms to be generated.

The private messages are used for updating, which is a private matter of the object.

The defined messages should be represented by diagrams of relationships between a caller and a receiver. The diagrams are important for the following reasons:

- Finding flaws in the design
- As a template for actual coding
- For debugging the system.

The set of drawings contains three specific types of drawings:

- For the system: the class hierarchy
- For each class: object dependences (data structures, and their relationships to other objects within the system)
- For each class: messages, and their flow in the system.

It is a good practice to sort alphabetically all of an object's derived classes. Object dependencies describe the structure of nested attributes (Fig. 9.4). If object A contains a reference in its element P to object B then there is a single dependency between objects A and B, through P. If the element P can sometimes contain a pointer to object B and sometimes a pointer to object C, than there is a multiple dependency. In Fig. 9.4 the attribute `Name` in class `Customer` can contain a pointer (i.e. an object identifier) to a string or a pointer to an object of type `PictureName`.

The message flow specifies accessing and sending messages by each object. The objective is not to illustrate all of the message flow throughout the complete system, simply the primary messages that are exchanged between objects. There are two kinds of message flow diagrams for each object. Diagrams showing all messages that can be sent and those showing all messages that can be accepted. In some cases they can be united into one diagram as in Fig. 9.5.

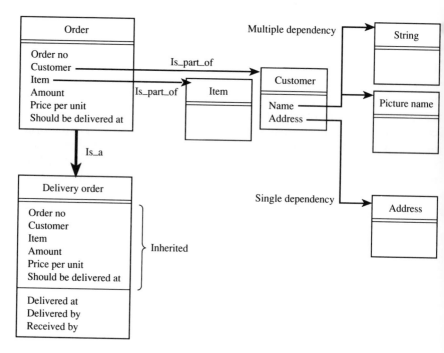

Figure 9.4 Class hierarchy.

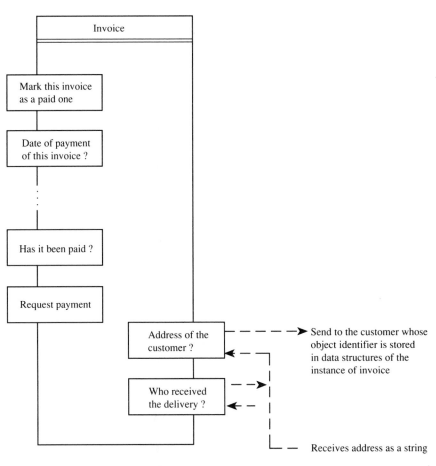

Figure 9.5 Message flow

PART
FOUR

IMPLEMENTATION OF AN OBJECT-ORIENTED DATABASE SYSTEM

TEN

IMPLEMENTATION TECHNIQUES

In this chapter we will focus on storage structures and implementation techniques used for objects such as occur in the main or disk memory. Access methods to these structures are related to problems of clustering and indexing and will be described in Chapter 11. Implementation techniques can only be given in outline here because object-oriented database systems are implemented in various languages and often use different concepts. In this and the following two chapters we will concentrate on the basic and interesting techniques used in implemented systems based on published experiences with GemStone, ORION, Iris.

10.1 THE ARCHITECTURE OF AN OODBMS

An OODBMS (Fig. 10.1) consists of the following encapsulated units:

1. Interface
2. Interpreter

- Message-processing subsystem
- Transaction-processing subsystem

3. Object manager

- Object subsystem
- Storage subsystem.

Depending on the type of client/server architecture used, these units are

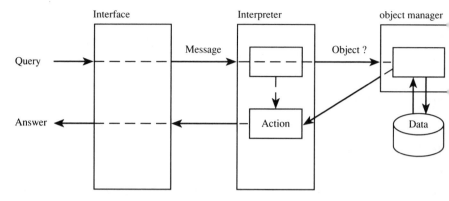

Figure 10.1 The architecture of an OODBMS

parts of the client process or the server process. In this book we use the page server architecture for our explanations. Evaluation of the advantages and disadvantages of different models of client/server architecture in the object-oriented environment is a topic of ongoing research.

The interface of an OODBMS offers possibilities of convenient problem-oriented formulation of queries and statements. Very often it will be based on a system of horizontal and vertical menus or on some more sophisticated screen graphics. This is a very important aspect of the database technology (not only for OODBMSs) because no one can expect that a designer, a bookkeeper or a stewardess will formulate their queries in OPAL language when using an object-oriented database built on GemStone.

The interpreter receives a message (Fig. 10.1) and checks its acceptability (i.e. provides a syntactic and semantic analysis). If this message is accepted the interpreter asks the object manager for the object given as the receiver of this message and then lets run the object's method which implements the message received. The role of the transaction management will be described in Chapter 12.

The object manager is responsible for physical data access and manipulation, i.e. for allocating objects on disk and organizing the transfer of data between disk and memory.

When implementing an object-oriented system we have to make a decision concerning implementation techniques for:

- Complex object representation
- Object identifiers
- Message passing
- Persistence
- Indexing
- Clustering
- Concurrency control and recovery

• Schema evolution, versions

We will begin with storage management where the representation of objects is the most important aspect.

10.2 IMPLEMENTATION STRUCTURES

10.2.1 The representation of objects on disk

In relational databases an object is represented by one record or (more often) by many. These records are either in a buffer in main memory or in a file on disk. Data structures in main memory and data structures on disk fit together. This is a major advantage of relational database systems. The problem, and principal drawback, is that many disk operations must be provided for assembling an object from many records which are spread throughout many files.

In object-oriented databases objects are stored on a heap in main memory. They have quite different sizes (often, instances of one class have different sizes) which can be dynamically changed. On the other hand, when using a disk file system we have only a set of pages of fixed length available. It is obvious that these data structures do not fit together. This is the source of many problems in implementation of OODBMSs. Efficient storage of objects and their retrieval on disk are the subject of research in many fields. Object-oriented languages support creating and using objects in main memory but not storing them on disk. Either they do not support this at all (like object-oriented versions of Pascal or C++) or not efficiently enough (like Smalltalk). It is, of course, possible to use a relational storage subsystem e.g., in Iris (Wilkinson *et al.*, 1990) but in this case we get the old disadvantages of the relational system, i.e. redundancy at the physical level and necessity of joins for assembling objects from their parts.

On computers where OODBMSs are running the disk space will be divided into partitions, segments, pages and blocks. Very often, the page size equals the block size, which implies that we get one page into main memory using one disk operation. To define a representation suitable for storage management, we have to define:

• How to represent an object
• How to store objects on a page.

In Fig. 10.2 we show the implementation of an object which was successfully used in ORION (Kim *et al.*, 1989).

This approach to the access to persistent data will be denoted as a two-level store approach. Two formats of references will be used here—

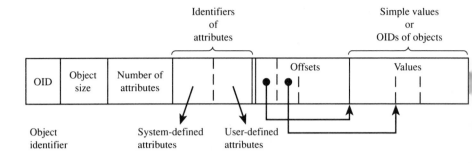

Figure 10.2 The instance representation

disk format and memory format (ORION, ONTOS). Other OODBMSs (GemStone, O_2) use a disk-based approach where persistent data in memory and transient data have different referencing. A method called one-level store uses for all data a virtual memory address space and maps persistent objects on disk (used in ObjectStore).

As we can see, the data structure representing an object consists of:

- Object identifier
- Object size
- Attribute count
- Description of system- and user-defined attributes
- Values offset vector
- Data values of attributes

The most important concept of the representation of instances is the concept of an object identifier (often abbreviated to OID). As mentioned in Chapter 3, each object has a system-generated unique object identifier in an object-oriented database.

Example
The object identifier OID will be called object-oriented pointer (OOP) in GemStone. This is a 32-bit signed integer generated by GemStone. We can arrange to print an 'object header' with each object when we use the message 'display oops' in the TOPAZ environment. In this case, we obtain for each object its OOP, its size and OOP of its class. A known OOP can be used to a direct access to the object when using a message object @OOP.

The first question concerning the object identifier is whether it has to contain the class identifier. Both approaches are used.

When the object identifier contains the class identifier then it is easy for the system to check whether the message sent matches one of the methods of the addressed object. For this checking it is not necessary to fetch the object (it can be stored on disk) because the class identifier can be extracted from the object identifier. This means that the object will be fetched only if the message is valid. The disadvantage of this approach is that it is expensive to change membership of objects in classes because all references to such an object have to be updated.

When the object identifier does not contain the class identifier then the class identifier must be stored as a system-defined attribute of the object. If it has to be checked when validating a message the object has to be fetched but when the object changes its class, only values of this attribute in all instances must be changed. This implies that if an object migrates from one class to another all references to the object remain valid since they have nothing in common with their class membership.

As shown in Fig. 10.2, single values are stored directly, composite values are stored indirectly, i.e. an object identifier is stored at the same place. To recognize where the values begin, an offset vector is used.

Each class defined in the system is also stored as an object. It consists of:

- Class attributes (shared by all instances of the class)
- Class methods (e.g. new)
- Instance attributes (names and structures)
- Instance methods (names and code)
- A reference to superclass
- References to all instances.

The schema of an object-oriented database is a set of system-defined and user-defined classes. The system classes `class`, `attribute` and `method` exist for this purpose. They not only maintain all information about all classes, attributes, and methods they also contain the aggregation mapping between classes and their attributes and methods and the generalization mapping between each class and its subclasses.

In Fig. 10.3 we see a possible implementation of object storing on a page. From the beginning of the page we store data concerned with the page, from the end of the page we store objects. This method is used very often when storing two dynamically changing structures into a memory space of fixed length (e.g. in compiling techniques for stack and heap). A page consists of four parts:

- Header (number of objects, total free space, contiguous free space, offset to free space)
- Indirect pointer array (relative address of objects on the page)
- Objects
- Free space for storing objects.

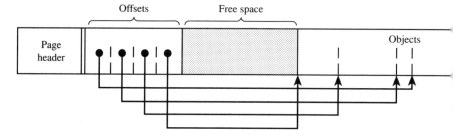

Figure 10.3 Objects on a disk page

Additional problems occur in cases where the size of the objects exceeds one page (e.g. for images stored as large bitmaps). Such objects are represented by a sequence of linked pages, e.g. in a B-tree structure. B-trees and hash tables keyed on object identifier are also used for implementation of sets. Sets are very important in object-oriented databases. They can represent very large collections of objects and their size may increase and decrease dynamically.

10.2.2 Representation of objects in the main memory

Access to objects in the main memory is based on the usage of the Resident Object Table (ROT). This is the table where the access manager having OID looks for the object. Figure 10.4 shows the organization of objects used in Smalltalk (Kaehler, 1981). There is a distinction here between object description, which is stored in a table called a Resident Object Description (ROD) table, and object data which is stored in the so-called object-buffer with heap organization.

The resident object table represents a mapping between values of OID and pointers to ROD tables for all objects which are stored in main memory. In addition to this mapping, the resident object table contains other useful information (not shown in Fig. 10.4), e.g. a bit indicating if some attribute values of this object have been changed. This is necessary for deciding whether the object should be copied back to the disk for saving its persistent data. Another useful column of the resident object table contains the time of the last operation on the object. This information will be used when the object buffer manager is looking for the least recently used object, which could be overwritten.

The resident object description table contains, in addition to the pointer to the object in the object buffer its OID, its physical object identifier (PID) specifying its disk address, a pointer to ROD-table of its class, and other details.

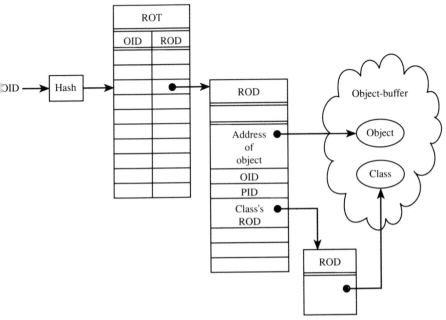

Figure 10.4 the object manager and resident object table

10.3 THE OBJECT MANAGEMENT

In every OODBMS there must be an object manager responsible for cases when:

- An object is requested, i.e. the object identifier is given and the object's address should be returned. There are two possibilities. The object is in the main memory and the sender of the request will obtain its address, or the requested object is not in the main memory. In the latter case the manager must find it on the disk, make some free space in the main memory, load it and return its address.
- A new object has been created, i.e. all constructors of all classes have to cooperate with the manager,
- There is not enough space in the main memory and some objects have to be moved to the disk.

The object manager must provide access to objects, both in the memory and on the disk. There are two kinds of buffers in an OODBMS (Figs 10.4, 10.5):

- Page buffer
- Object buffer.

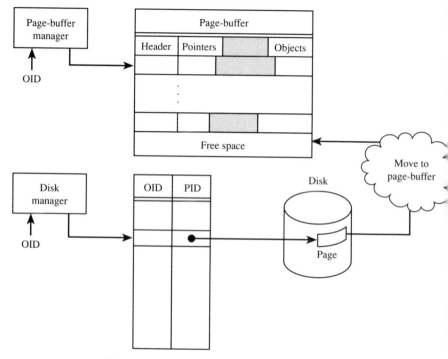

Figure 10.5 Page-buffer manager and disk manager

Thus an object can be found in the object buffer (directly accessible via ROT, ROD), in the page buffer (indirectly accessible but without a disk operation) or on the disk (indirectly accessible using a disk operation for loading a page into page buffer). The object manager is responsible for these operations. It has three subordinates (Fig. 10.6):

- A page-buffer manager
- An object-buffer manager
- A disk manager.

The object manager maintains the resident object table ROT.

When an application needs an object the object manager will obtain the identifier of this object and is expected to return a pointer to a descriptor resident object descriptor (ROD) of the object wanted. To perform this operation it calls its subordinate object-buffer manager which maintains the resident object table (ROT). The object-manager uses a hash function to get an index into the ROT-table from the OID. If it succeeds, it sends the object descriptor's pointer that it finds to the object manager. If it does not succeed, it follows that the requested object is not in the object-buffer. When the object manager receives such a message it calls the page-buffer manager with the task of finding the requested object.

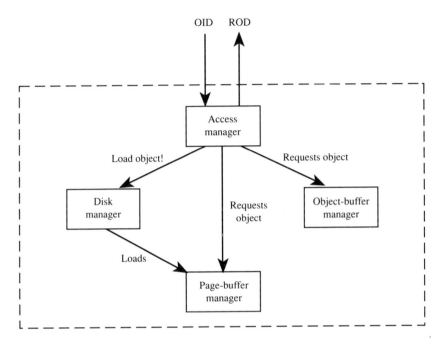

Figure 10.6 Storage subsystem of the object manager

This object can be in some page in the page-buffer which it shares with other objects requested previously. If this is not the case, then the storage manager will be called. It has a table OID-PID available which represents the complete mapping of all objects in the database in the disk space (PID). Using a hashing method, the storage manager finds the physical address of the requested object and loads the relevant page into the page-buffer. Then the page-buffer manager will load the object from the page-buffer into the object-buffer and complete the ROT table. Finally, the object-buffer manager will find the pointer of the object descriptor in the ROT table and return it to the object manager.

In the object descriptor ROD there is also a pointer to the object in the object buffer. This is how the application will obtain access to values stored in the object requested.

ELEVEN

INDEXING TECHNIQUES

The performance enhancement of query processing depends on access methods used for retrieval of objects concerned in queries. There are three main possibilities for improving the efficiency of querying:

- Query optimization
- Clustering
- Indexing.

Query optimization is an important part (and often a standard part) of relational DBMSs, whereas in OODBMSs it is subject to research and is beyond the scope of this book. In this chapter we will discuss clustering and indexing which can be denoted as access methods.

Before discussing access methods we will show the data structure which are under discussion. In Fig. 11.1 we have two kinds of links:

- Subclass links represent the relationship *Is_a* and specify the inheritance in the class hierarchy.
- Domain links represent the relationship *Is_part_of* and specify the composition of objects.

In access methods we can then address single classes, the structure given by subclass links, or the structure given by domain links. In this way access methods can also be divided.

11.1 CLUSTERING

In the logical design of a relational database we do not solve the problem of physical storing of tables. We accept the abstraction—somewhere on disk. Nevertheless, it is very important for purposes of performance and

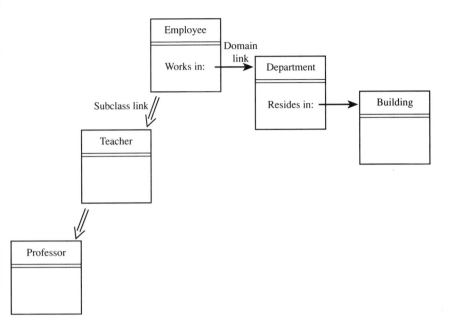

Figure 11.1 Class-hierarchy indexing in OODBMS

efficiency to design not only logical structures but also physical structures, i.e. to design how the database tables will be mapped into files, pages, cylinders, etc. By a page, we mean here an amount of data that can be transferred from disk to memory by one I/O operation. It can be also called a physical block.

Clustering is a method used in some relational DBMSs (e.g. in ORACLE) for grouping rows of tables with the aim of placing frequently co-referenced objects near to each other in the sense of disk organization due to reducing the number of I/O operations required for query processing. Without clustering, the statement `insert` stores newly appended rows of the table into the disk space after each other in the order they are entered. This means that the rows stored on one page may have only one property in common, namely that they have been entered in a given time period. This can be useful (e.g. for invoices) but often we prefer another physical ordering. Clustering can be used for:

- Data from one table
- Data from more tables.

When we define clustering for one table, we specify an attribute (a column of the table), values of which will be used for deciding to which cluster the row belongs. Such a cluster will be stored on one page or

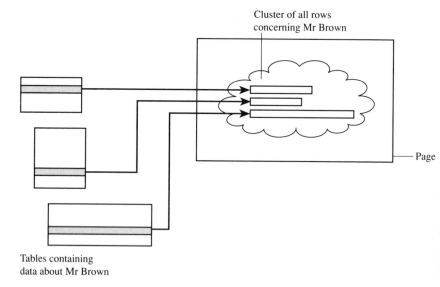

Cluster of all rows
concerning Mr Brown

Page

Tables containing
data about Mr Brown

Figure 11.2 Clustering data from more tables

on one cylinder to achieve the minimal amount of disk operations for retrieval.

Example

We have a table `cars` where a row is appended when a car is bought. The order of a row on the disk pages depends on the date of the sale transaction. If we often need to look up all yellow cars then we will define a clustering given by the column `colour`. In this case, we can find all the yellow cars with a minimal number of disk accesses.

Clustering for more-tables data (Fig. 11.2) brings these rows from more tables into one page together which often occur in joins. This means that properties of one object can be spread into more tables but they will be physically stored in such clusters where each cluster includes rows of different tables concerning one object.

Clustering in OODBMSs includes both cases shown above and, in addition, cases derived from inheritance and from composition of objects, i.e.:

- Clustering instances of one class
- Clustering all instances of one class which have a given property
- Clustering instances with respect to the class-hierarchy structure
- Clustering instances with respect to the nested-attribute structure

- Clustering instances where classes build a subgraph of the database schema.

Finding the best clustering is an NP-problem (i.e. there is no procedure that could find the solution). In practice, queries will be audited, statistically evaluated and the DBMS will be tuned. Tuning means that its clustering and also other properties dependent on the physical storage organization will be changed with the aim of improving performance. If this process is performed automatically, we call it dynamic clustering (CACTIS (Hudson and King, 1986)). This can be a very useful concept in applications where read operations are dominant.

An OODBMS should support the following operations concerning clusters:

- Create a cluster
- Add an object to a cluster
- Drop a cluster
- Change an object's membership of a cluster.

When constructing clusters we have to know how the inherited attributes are stored. There are principally two possibilities:

- Attributes of an object are described on different levels but all their values are stored at the lowest level of the inheritance tree (ORION (Banerjee *et al.*, 1987b)).
- Attributes of an object are not only described they are also stored spread in the class-hierarchy tree (Iris (Fishman *et al.*, 1989)).

The first strategy seems to be more practical because the second offers, on the one hand, minimal storage overheads (the common values of attributes are stored only once) and, on the other, the retrieval of an instance also requires a multiple join operation in order to get all properties of an object together. This depends, of course, on the queries used. Applications exist where an object is never needed as a whole.

Because of the existence of complex objects we can do clustering in two ways:

- Breadth-first clustering
- Depth-first clustering.

They differ in the way the algorithms of object instance variables clustering traverse the tree structure which represents the domain link hierarchy (Fig. 11.3). In the breadth-first strategy (Fig. 11.3b) the algorithm tries to backtrack after each forward step. In the depth-first strategy (Fig. 11.3a) the algorithm backtracks only if necessary, i.e. only if a leaf in the traversed tree has been reached.

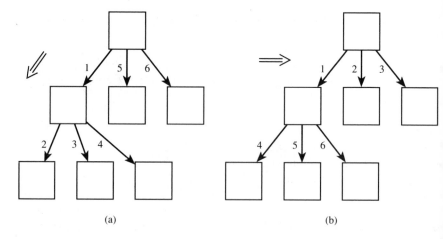

(a)   (b)

Figure 11.3 Strategies of clustering composed objects (a) depth-first; (b) breadth-first

11.1.1. Clustering in GemStone

In GemStone there is a universal message `cluster` for assigning an object (the receiver of this message) to a disk page. More precisely, the OID of an object will be assigned without any attempt to cluster the instance variables of this object. To do this, a method must be written which clusters instance variables using the depth-first or the breadth-first strategy.

Example
Using the breadth-first strategy in Fig. 11.3 we obtain the following clustering:

```
OID-Teacher OID-Code-Id    OID-Name       OID-Address
OID-Salary  OID-First-Name OID-Last-Name OID-Street
OID-House   OID-Town
```

Using the depth-first strategy in Fig. 11.3 we obtain:

```
OID-Teacher    OID-Code-Id OID-Name       OID-First-Name
OID-Last-Name OID-Address OID-Street    OID-House
OID-Town       OID-Salary
```

Pages are used in a page stream, which means that when a page is